I0759530

Tapping Into You

TRANSFORM TRAUMA & REDISCOVER YOUR INNER POWER THROUGH EFT

Sarah Tobin

To Alice Rose Frances Tobin,
my guiding light, forever in my heart.

First published in Great Britain in 2025
by Godsfield, an imprint of
Octopus Publishing Group Ltd
Carmelite House
50 Victoria Embankment
London EC4Y 0DZ
www.octopusbooks.co.uk
www.octopusbooksusa.com

An Hachette UK Company
www.hachette.co.uk

The authorized representative in the EEA is Hachette Ireland, 8 Castlecourt Centre, Dublin 15, D15 XTP3, Ireland (email: info@hbgi.ie)

Distributed in the US by Hachette Book Group, 1290 Avenue of the Americas, 4th and 5th Floors, New York, NY 10104

Distributed in Canada by Canadian Manda Group, 664 Annette Street, Toronto, Ontario, Canada M6S 2C8

ISBN 978-1-84181-619-7

A CIP catalogue record for this book is available from the British Library.

Printed and bound in China.

10 9 8 7 6 5 4 3 2 1

Commissioning Editor: Louisa Johnson
Art Director: Juliette Norsworthy
Senior Editor: Leanne Bryan
Copy Editor: Chloe Murphy
Designer: Nikki Ellis
Illustrator: Ella McLean
Assistant Production Manager:
Allison Gonsalves

Publisher's note
All reasonable care has been taken in the preparation of this book but the information it contains is not intended to take the place of treatment by a qualified medical practitioner.

Before making any changes to your health regime, always consult a doctor. While all the therapies detailed in this book are completely safe if done correctly, you must seek professional advice if you are in any doubt about any medical condition. Any application of the ideas and information contained in this book is at the reader's sole discretion and risk.

Contents

Introduction

This book exists as a result of pain, loss and trauma.

Ever since finding tapping, I knew it was my purpose to share it with as many people as possible, and writing a book was always part of this vision and dream. This book isn't about my trauma itself; it is about the modality that saved me.

Unfortunately, we all experience trauma, and too often we are left to fend for ourselves, picking up the pieces of our broken heart and finding a way to live with the pain. This is surviving at its best. But I don't believe we are here just to survive. My heart tells me we are here to thrive, create, love, share, speak our truth and find joy, even as we experience the hardships in life.

Life gives us the opportunity to experience everything and to let go, move on, withstand, learn and grow, just as nature does all around us.

WE ARE HERE TO THRIVE, CREATE, LOVE, SHARE, SPEAK OUR TRUTH AND FIND JOY.

My Story

I'm sharing my story for context, and I've made this short to reduce the chance of triggering you, just in case you unfortunately can relate to this experience.

Our daughter Alice Rose Frances Tobin was born full term in November 2014 after a beautifully uncomplicated pregnancy. During the final stages of her birth, she somehow did not get the oxygen she needed. It was identified too late, and she was placed on a cooling pad in the neonatal unit for 72 hours to see if she had a chance to recover. Unfortunately, the brain damage was too great, and after an MRI confirmed this on day five, we made the decision to let her go. I feel I've been learning to let go and surrender ever since.

Luckily, I got pregnant five months later, but was suffering from undiagnosed severe post-traumatic stress disorder (PTSD) at the time. I had gone back to work and was having horrific flashbacks, felt incredibly anxious and was scared about the upcoming birth. It was at this time that I discovered the lifeline of tapping that completely transformed my PTSD, eased my broken heart, helped me gain acceptance of our loss and prepared me for my upcoming birth.

The discovery of tapping changed my life in so many ways. It significantly aided my trauma recovery, and the process of becoming an emotional freedom technique (EFT) practitioner and subsequent EFT sessions made me realize that I was a highly-functioning anxious person, totally disconnected from my body, not living my true purpose, and had no clue who I was at my core. I was not being my true and authentic self. Tapping was the catalyst and modality that has made me more spiritual, authentic, fulfilled, present, joyful and trusting of myself and the universe.

I acknowledge that I am perfectly imperfect. I have made and will continue to make mistakes because I am human. I have let go of the need for perfection, and maybe you will, too.

What is Tapping?

Tapping, or emotional freedom technique, is a somatic therapy that involves physically tapping on specific points on the body (as influenced by acupuncture and acupressure) while simultaneously voicing your current emotions, focusing on negative ones. It is a combination of Eastern medicine and Western psychology, and brings together elements of exposure, cognitive therapy and somatic stimulation.

While tapping the 14 tapping points (see page 32), you are sending electromagnetic pulses through the energy field via neurotransmitters. This signals safety to the amygdala near the centre of the brain, which in turn switches off the body's stress response, gently guiding it back into relaxation mode.

This brain hack is a signal of calm, love and comfort. You are telling the body to feel safe in the current moment, whether you are currently navigating a difficult time or you are recalling something traumatic from the past.

This feeling of safety will allow your body to relax, and you might feel your breath deepen and release a big sigh. I'll explain more about tapping and how to do it in Chapter 3.

THIS BRAIN HACK IS A SIGNAL OF CALM, LOVE AND COMFORT.

The Power of Tapping

A few years ago in London, I received devastating news about my former boss, which closely mirrored a personal tragedy I had experienced. The timing could not have been worse as I was just about to enter a day-long meeting. Throughout the meeting, my body was present, but my mind and emotions were in turmoil, making it incredibly difficult to focus. As soon as the meeting ended, I boarded the tube, and the pent-up sadness began to overflow in the form of silent tears.

In the privacy of a station bathroom, the emotional pain became overwhelming. Feeling like I was reliving the trauma, I began tapping on my head and followed the EFT tapping sequence, repeating affirmations such as 'This isn't happening to me' and 'I am safe'. Although I could not reach a neutral or positive state, within three minutes I felt the intensity of my emotions decrease from a 10 to a 7. I was then able to compose myself and catch my train, and later that evening I continued tapping to process my emotions further.

Guidance on Using This Book

1

When you are tapping along with me, you can use your own words and tune in to your personal memories and circumstances. The more specific you are, the better the results will be. Start by copying my words to gain confidence, and then repeat the exercise adding in your own.

2

If at any point you feel overwhelmed with intense emotion, open your eyes, take some deep breaths and keep tapping 'I am safe' for a round or two. Bring your awareness into your body and senses by considering what you can see, touch, hear, smell and taste. Remind yourself that you are safe: it's safe to feel these emotions and it's safe to let them go.

3

If memories come up, make a note of them in a journal, and for big and long-standing traumas, I would recommend working with an EFT practitioner in person or online to support you. Big traumas can include a car crash; abuse; neglect or separation from Mum (especially in early childhood); emotional or physical bullying; baby loss; birth trauma; loss of a parent or sibling; and much more. See Chapter 3 for further support on what to do if memories surface.

Before We Begin

I invite you to assess your sense of self-worth and self-love by rating each of them as percentages out of 100. Write them down somewhere, and I'll ask you at the end of the book to do the same again. Pay attention to cues provided by your mind, body and soul that can indicate shifts and changes as you move through the exercises and the letting go process.

Thank you so much for letting me guide you on this journey home to your authentic self. It is an honour to share this with you. This is a starting point and something I hope will become a lifelong practice and tool that you can use anytime and anywhere to support yourself. My wish for you is that you start to see tapping as a really effective emotion and stress management tool, and that it helps you to find your way home, just as it did for me.

Love,

Sarah Tobin

STEP 1:
LAYING THE FOUNDATION

We begin our journey with the essential groundwork: reconnecting with the unconditional love and worth that is innate to us all. This first step is an invitation to recognize the importance of the energy and frequency within and around us. As you read, you'll learn the basics of tapping, a simple, effective tool to help align your body and mind for healing and resilience. Together, we're setting a solid foundation of awareness and self-compassion to prepare for the transformative work that lies ahead.

CHAPTER 1

Understanding Your Soul Power

The process of remembering your authentic self can take time.

Soul Power

Do you know who you are? Who are you really at your core? Deep within us, we have a power. I call it soul power, and it is something divinely created within you at the moment of your soul's creation, and is the energy of unconditional love (which we'll discuss more in Chapter 16).

This is your life force energy. It shapes you and every living being on this earth, but the thing is, we are born with a little amnesia and a lack of awareness of this amazing life force energy. Some children are very aware of this energy, and consciously connect to it and the unseen realms of our universe. However, often we experience trauma, pain and suffering that disconnects us from this source of love, and we can feel abandoned and separated from that love as a result because we don't understand the bigger picture. This can lead us to make limited judgements about ourselves, other people and the world around us.

Remembering

Through pain and trauma, we develop strategies to protect ourselves, and we may even erect an invisible wall around our hearts to prevent us from being hurt again.

The process of remembering our authentic selves can take time. Although tapping is not necessarily quick, it can speed this process up. The layers that have been created over time need to be lovingly, compassionately and carefully released. You can think of it like an onion with all the layers, leading to a central core. This core is your soul power (your true self), and these outer layers were created for protection.

Tapping can introduce the safety required to aid the letting go and remembering process.

Your purpose in life is to remember, to tap into you and to find out who you really are beneath all the layers that represent the traumas, beliefs, conditions and expectations of others.

This book will support your healing journey so that you can get to know who you are and what you want, as well as how to express yourself without masks; create positive boundaries; find the courage to be vulnerable and fully accepting of yourself; and connect to that beautiful well of unconditional love waiting for you to remember.

Discovering My Purpose

The act of remembering and healing reveals the hidden talents, gifts and wisdom that you've come here to experience and share. The loss of Alice cracked me open so painfully that I was desperate to find something to help. Tapping helped profoundly, but it also brought me something else. It awakened a desire in me to help others who were suffering in the way I had been helped. I had always felt that I wasn't living my true purpose in corporate marketing and had been searching for ways out. My own healing shone the light, and I followed my intuition and strong inner guidance every step of the way.

I love being the detective and helping people understand their life by piecing together the puzzle, and following the threads to core beliefs they need to release. I get such a buzz from teaching and sharing what I've learned with others and now I'm feeling fulfilled by writing. All these gifts came from the depths of trauma, and most importantly from my pathway of healing from darkness to the light.

Soul Versus Ego

The term 'alignment' is a spiritual term used to indicate being on track and in flow. In this state, there is minimal resistance, and energy and abundance flow to you. You may even find yourself feeling happy, joyful and content most of the time. When in alignment, the soul is in charge of the mind and ego, working to support the soul's dreams and desires.

When out of alignment, the mind steps in and assumes control. During a negative experience or trauma, the mind and body feel unsafe. This is where the ego takes over, because it is tasked with keeping you safe. Often in these situations, the soul's voice quietens, and although it is always a part of you, it can feel distant and disconnected, almost like it's had a fright. We can feel detached from our emotions and not recognize what we are feeling. The ego's voice can be loud, restrictive and sometimes downright nasty. Often this happens when we are young, and we don't even notice how overpowering and limiting it is. You'll learn more about the ego on pages 143–4.

The book will help you to increase your awareness of and improve your relationship with your critical voice, as working with the ego in this way will allow it to step back, and let the mind, body and soul realign.

THE EGO TAKES OVER BECAUSE IT IS TASKED WITH KEEPING YOU SAFE.

Inner Reflection

Deep healing takes inner reflection and awareness. No one else can do this for you, but you can be guided. You are reading these words because your highest self brought you to this place, and this book has arrived at the perfect time for you on your journey of remembering. Allow yourself to set an intention now for the journey you are undertaking or continuing.

SET YOUR TAPPING INTENTION

- *First, tune in to your heart space by placing a hand on your heart and taking some deep breaths.*
- *Imagine your heart expanding and contracting with each breath. Perhaps visualize a jellyfish pulsing.*
- *Focus on taking five inhales and five exhales to bring your body systems into harmony.*
- *Pick up a pen and piece of paper or a journal. Write an intention that can support you while reading this book and taking this journey, such as, 'I choose to embark on this journey with an open heart and mind'.*

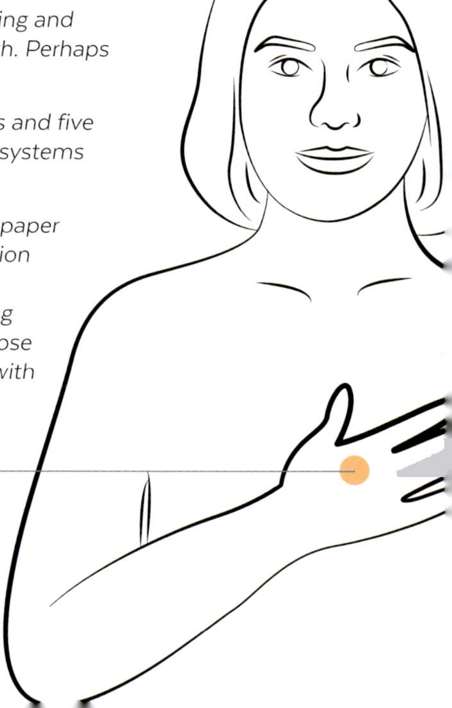

We Are Born Enough

This journey back to your authentic self is an opportunity to recognize your own worth and value, and to start to love yourself deeply. As you go inward on your journey – acknowledging your layers, validating your experiences, giving yourself compassion and forgiving yourself and/or others – you are loving yourself deeply.

So many of us feel unlovable and unworthy because of the pains and traumas we've experienced. We've made sense of them by inferring our lack of value, doubting our own abilities, believing we are not enough and building protective heart walls. But what if we reframe this? What if we are worthy simply because we exist, regardless of what we experience and what we make that mean?

The truth is that every single one of us is worthy, loveable and enough. No one person is more worthy than another. We are worthy simply because we exist in the web of life, and the energy we create and share with others through the web matters.

EVERY SINGLE ONE OF US IS WORTHY, LOVEABLE AND ENOUGH.

Picture your baby self or think about your own child. Could you imagine seeing this baby and thinking they are not worthy, or not enough in some way? Of course not. Let's take a moment to think about your inner child and send them love and appreciation. We also will look at this in more depth in Chapter 10, pages 113–15.

ADDRESS YOUR WORTHINESS

Close your eyes and visualize the start of your life here on Earth. See, sense or feel a bubble of light in front of you that is holding your baby self in utero.

Project unconditional love from your heart into the baby's heart. See this as a beautiful colour filling your baby self up, and expand it into the bubble so that the baby is floating in unconditional love.

Send thoughts to the baby such as, 'You are perfect just as you are', 'You are worthy', 'You are enough', 'You are loved' and any other loving words your little self needs to hear.

See the divine light and love within your baby self and watch it grow and expand, opening their heart as they receive this love with ease and grace.

Return to this exercise any time you feel you need a self-love boost, or feel unworthy or unlovable.

SOUL POWER MEDITATION

Find somewhere quiet and comfortable.

Close your eyes and take a few deep breaths to settle into this moment.

Imagine walking in a spiral shape from the outside to the inside, and that each step you take brings you one step closer to meeting the soul power within you.

With each step, imagine there is an unravelling, shedding and releasing. You could envisage this as energy leaving through your feet with every step. With each step, also imagine that love is coming in through the crown of your head or directly into your heart, as you grow and expand into higher and lighter energies.

Continue walking in a spiral shape for as long as you wish. There is no final destination, because your true self is with you the whole time, it's just being revealed or brought into the light as you walk.

To close, repeat the following affirmations three times: I am worthy. I am enough. I am loved.

CHAPTER 2

Tuning into Energies

Tapping is the perfect tool to send signals that disperse low-frequency energy and release it from the body, allowing us to connect with high-vibrational energy instead.

Everything is Energy

The terms vibration and frequency are being used more and more to describe our energy. When we look into the detail of all things, everything is made up of atoms: you, me and the crystals on my desk. Atoms are formed by electromagnetic waves that have a specific frequency. And when atoms come together to form things, there is a combined frequency output of that object or person.

Frequency can be described as a unit of measurement for vibration. The electromagnetic waves are not static and are vibrating and moving constantly. Frequency measures how many vibration cycles complete in one second.

Our physical, emotional and mental health is impacted by frequency. When we feel emotionally drained, low, burdened or stressed, our frequency is lower compared to when we feel joyful, calm and grateful. That is because emotions are energy in motion, and they each have their own frequency.

Our frequency is like a signal that connects us consciously and unconsciously to the world around us. You can also feel it from objects and places. Have you ever walked into a house or room and felt that you could cut the tension with a knife? Or alternatively, walked into a space and felt it is immediately healing, grounding and peaceful?

EMOTIONS ARE ENERGY IN MOTION.

The Quantum Field

In quantum physics, the quantum field is viewed as a fundamental entity permeating all of space, which lays the groundwork for everything from star formation and physical objects to our deepest relationships and personal healing. This field is a dynamic, interconnected web of energy and information that shapes our physical reality.

Max Planck, the father of quantum theory, proposed that what we see, touch and experience are not the true bases of reality. Rather, our consciousness, our awareness, thoughts and perceptions form the real foundation.[1] This perspective underpins both the Law of Attraction and general manifesting techniques, which suggest that our thoughts help create our experiences. Our frequency interacts continuously with the quantum field, sending out signals that reflect our feelings and beliefs, which in turn draw corresponding people, things and circumstances into our lives.

Our Energy Field

It is widely accepted that we have our own personal electromagnetic field that surrounds and permeates our physical body, known as our aura or energy field. It is said to consist of various layers such as the physical, emotional, mental and spiritual. This energy field also contains our seven major chakras, which are specific and concentrated centres of energy in our bodies.

Emotional disturbances and blockages are not just felt in the physical body, but are also reflected in the aura. When we actively release and let go of emotions, we are clearing the blockages in the energy field so that natural order and flow can be restored.

The Seven Chakras

Why Does Energy Matter?

Energy is never constant, as the nature of energy is movement, with atoms infinitely vibrating. This is great news for us on our healing journeys because it means we can change.

We can impact our frequency through our thoughts, emotions, behaviours and interactions with other high frequency atoms. As we shift our emotional state from low-frequency energy associated with fear, guilt and shame, we raise our vibration to higher vibrational frequencies such as joy, love and peace.

Guilt and shame are some of the heaviest and densest energies we can carry. Often these aren't even ours; we have inherited them from our family, religion and society. Liberating ourselves from these heavy energies will bring a great sense of relief and also free us up to connect with higher frequency energies that allow us to enjoy life more. Tapping is the perfect tool to send signals that disperse and release low frequency energy from the body, allowing us to connect with this higher vibrational energy instead.

Our Thoughts Impact Our Frequency

Like emotions, our thoughts also have their own individual frequencies. Thoughts we have and words we speak or read can make us feel good, or not so good. We can all relate to hearing our critical voice loud and clear and the impact that it has on our feelings as well as our subsequent actions.

Jean Piaget's theory of cognitive development[2] tells us that by the age of seven or eight, we have developed the core belief structure or mindset that stays with us for the rest of our lives (unless we do very conscious reprogramming work, such as reading this book).

Every experience we have from in utero and beyond is analyzed by our subconscious mind for threat or danger.

According to psychology professor Paul Rozin and lecturer in behavioural sciences Edward Royzman,[3] we are negatively biased to interpret the negative aspect of experiences in order to shape safety strategies that keep us safe in the future. This means that adverse events have more of an impact on our psychological state than positive ones, so even if we have more positive events overall, we feel the impact of the negative experiences more.

Our subconscious is a clever system that focuses on survival over happiness and wellbeing, working hard to extract meaning from daily life. This happens especially in our early years, and it has more weight and impact due to our brainwave state, which is in Alpha state from the ages of five to eight, where we accept what we are told as truth, and soak everything up like a sponge.

Once a belief is formed, it is used as a filter through which we view and make meaning of our future experiences. We seek to attract and affirm these beliefs, meaning we will interpret future experiences based on that filter, and affirm the belief was the right one in a 'I told you so' kind of way. Even if the truth was something else entirely, it's how we interpret our experiences that makes the difference.

This safety system also shapes our actions. But decisions that were once solutions can become controlling, almost like an invisible, self-imposed prison. Often referred to as 'limiting beliefs', as adults, they can become the unseen or subconscious block that limits our manifestations and desired outcomes. This weds us to the past, making it more difficult to move forward with the ability to create the life we want. We are held back from being inspired and connected to our true, authentic and divine self.

It is easy to understand how a four-year-old who experiences a mild car crash might interpret the experience as not safe, which can lead to the belief, 'The world's not a safe place' or, 'I am not safe', or result in the decision, 'I'm never leaving home because it is not safe outside'. Fortunately, our thought patterns are not fixed; interpretations can shift, beliefs can be released and new, empowering decisions can be made.

FUTURE SELF MEDITATION

There is a version of you in the future living the life of your dreams. You can meet with them any time you choose for love and compassion, wisdom and guidance or simply to hang out.

During this meditation, you may like to have some crystals with you, diffuse some essential oils such as frankincense or jasmine, or play some relaxing music like 852 Hz Solfeggio frequencies (see page 68).

You will need a journal and a pen.

1. *Start by connecting to your breath. Just notice it at first then, after a few moments, start to regulate the length of your inhalations and exhalations, breathing in to the count of five, then breathing out to the count of five.*
2. *Set an intention to connect with your future self and allow yourself to be open to what you see, sense or feel during this visualization.*
3. *Focus on your heart centre. Perhaps you can imagine yourself breathing in and out of your heart the same way a jellyfish moves with its beautiful pulsing flow. See a golden light in your heart.*
4. *Imagine that you are hovering over a timeline on the ground. Behind you is a line indicating your past, and in front of you is a line indicating your future. You are hovering over this precious and present day. You notice a spark of light in the distant future. It beckons you, drawing you closer. Your awareness is now moving down the timeline to greet this spark of light.*

5. *When you arrive at this light, you recognize a future version of yourself. They take you by the hand and you both move down toward the earth together. You land on the earth and take some time to notice your surroundings. Where are you? Let yourself drink in this future world that is waiting for you.*
6. *Imagine your future self smiles and greets you warmly, and takes you to a place where you can connect properly. Now is your chance to ask them questions and absorb their wisdom and guidance. Take as long as you like to sense what this future version of your life feels like.*
7. *Once you've spent enough time with your future self, express your gratitude and love for this version of you, and know you can come back to meet them at any time. Before they go, they give you a symbol or token of their existence to use as a sign from them when you need it.*
8. *When you're ready, imagine your future self guiding you upward, where they say goodbye. You float backward down the timeline, back to this present moment. The light of your future self gets smaller by the second, and you finally arrive back in the present and return fully into your body.*
9. *Take a few breaths and start to move your body.*
10. *Journal about your experience so you have something to look back on and add to as you repeat this practice in future.*

CHAPTER 3

How to Tap

Tapping is the most effective self-help tool, right at our fingertips.

How Tapping Affects Us

Tapping blends modern science with ancient wisdom. This powerful energy psychology and somatic therapy gently rewires our stress response and supports deep emotional healing, right down to our core traumas and limiting beliefs. With each tapping session we complete, we gain access to our inner resilience, allow ourselves to let go and restore natural healing. This is an act of self-love and complements a remembering of who you are at your core.

WITH EACH TAPPING SESSION WE COMPLETE, WE GAIN ACCESS TO OUR INNER RESILIENCE.

Where Did Tapping Come From?

Tapping originated from a modality called Thought Field Therapy (TFT), created by Dr Roger Callahan in the 1980s. Dr Callahan was a psychologist who was working with kinesiology and Chinese medicine, and understood that different parts of the body linked to organs and the production of the stress hormones cortisol and adrenaline.

In the early 1990s Gary Craig, a trained Stanford University engineer, coach and neuro-linguistic programming (NLP) master practitioner, heard of TFT and set out to investigate. Impressed with the therapy, he trained and studied directly with Dr Callahan and, after some investigation and experimentation, realized that tapping on all of the points (see page 32) in a simple top-down sequence produced the same effect as TFT. Today, this is what we know as EFT.

How Does EFT Work?

Whenever we perceive a threat to our physical safety or to our sense of self, the autonomic sympathetic nervous system kicks into gear and triggers the fight, flight, freeze or fawn (people pleasing) response. This activates our adrenal glands, producing the stress hormones cortisol and adrenaline, which prepare us to cope with or escape the perceived danger.

We are meant to use the sympathetic nervous system in short sharp bursts to support immediate threats. After the threat disappears, the body moves back into the parasympathetic nervous system response, otherwise known as 'rest and digest'. This state is where the body heals and rebalances itself.

Nowadays, however, we are all living in an elevated state of stress, with very few dips in our cortisol and adrenaline production. According to the Mayo Clinic,[1] prolonged cortisol and adrenaline in the bloodstream can put us at risk of many health conditions, such as anxiety; autoimmune disorders; cardiovascular disease; depression; digestive issues; headaches; insomnia; memory and concentration impairment; muscle tension and pain; strokes; and weight gain.

Tapping sends signals to the amygdala through the central nervous system, overriding the stress response and telling the brain to switch back to rest and digest.

What Can Tapping Help With?

The opportunities with tapping are far-reaching. You can tap on any and every topic or issue, and tapping has been proven to be an effective tool for managing addiction and cravings; anxiety; negative emotions such as anger, guilt or shame; PTSD; phobias and fears; stress; and trauma. It has also been used to aid memory, boost confidence levels and self-esteem and improve relationships with oneself and others.

Tapping can also help to reduce physical pain in the body, such as headaches, period pain and back or neck pain, by helping to release tension held in the muscles or energy blockages that may be causing pain. It does this by working on the emotional issues underlying the physical disease and disharmony presenting in the body as pain or other symptoms.

The Science

Over four thousand studies on EFT have been conducted as of 2024, and a paper that reviewed 139 English papers concluded that EFT treatment is effective for (a) psychological conditions such as anxiety, depression, phobias and PTSD; (b) physiological issues such as pain, insomnia and autoimmune conditions; (c) professional and sports performance; and (d) biological markers of stress. Meta-analyses evaluating the effect of EFT treatment have found this to be 'moderate' to 'large'.

A primary indicator of EFT's impact is its ability to reduce cortisol levels in the bloodstream. Research done in 2020 and 2022 by clinical and health psychologist Dr Peta Stapleton and her colleagues[2] set out to discover the impact of tapping on cortisol in the body, replicating research that had been conducted by science writer Dawson Church, published in 2012[3]. The research consisted of three groups: one who received an hour of EFT in a group setting; one who received a supportive listening session; and a control group who received nothing.

Cortisol levels dropped in the first group who received the tapping by 43 per cent. The second group had a reduction of 19 per cent and the third group's cortisol levels remained the same. This result shows how effective EFT is for reducing significant stress markers and demonstrates what a powerful tool it is for stress management and improving emotional wellbeing and physical health as a result.

How to Tap

There are four simple steps to tapping, which are explained on the following pages:

1. Tune in and rate how you are feeling
2. Create your set-up statement
3. Tap the points using your reminder statement
4. Check in and keep tapping

These are the points that we use in tapping:

ToH: Top of the head
EB: Start of the eyebrow
SoE: Side of the eye
UE: Under the eye
UN: Under the nose
CH: Chin
CB: Collarbones
UA: Under the arm
IW: Inner Wrist
TH: Thumb
FF: Forefinger
MF: Middle finger
RF: Ring finger
BF: Baby finger

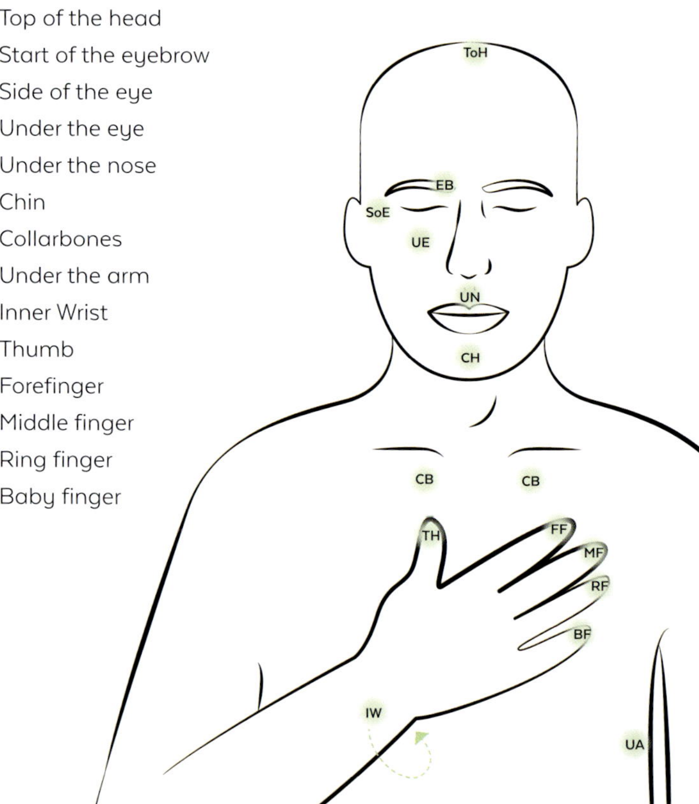

Start tapping at the top of the head and work your way down the body to under the upper arm, and then to the wrist and hands. I use the hand points because they were part of the original teachings, and I find that they can be useful and discreet in certain situations where a bit of stress relief would be welcome, such as in meetings or exams.

Tap five to seven times, or for the duration of the sentence you vocalize, at each tapping point (see pages 6 and 38). You can use one hand or two, on the left or right side of your body, and you can tap firmly or softly. This is a very forgiving tool, so don't worry if you miss a point every now and again.

NOTE:

None of the clinical EFT tapping trials and research uses the hand points, so this can be done with or without the hands. I use them every time I tap, so I've included them in the tapping sequences in this book. I have also suggested four rounds of tapping in most cases; however this is just a guide to get you started. Please feel free to tap as many rounds as it takes to feel a positive shift in your energy and emotions.

1. Tune In and Rate How You Are Feeling

The first step to tapping is to identify how you feel. This means tuning in to the sensations and tension in your body. Sometimes it is really easy to tune in; you might be crying so you feel sadness in your heart, or you might be panicking and feel anxiety in your stomach. Other times, feelings may be harder to identify because you have disconnected from your body and your emotions. Don't worry. If that's the case, when you set out to do some tapping, you'll be drawn to do it because something feels off, even if you can't identify what. You can still proceed and, as you tap, you may become more connected with and aware of your body and emotions.

Think about the energy you are connecting with in your body. It could be an emotion or a physical pain. Where is that energy in your body? It might even be in multiple locations.

What colour is the energy? If you struggle with this, just guess, as there is no right or wrong answer. For example, it could be heavy navy responsibility on my shoulders; red anger in my throat; or sharp black pain in my hip.

THE PURPOSE OF TUNING IN IS TO CONNECT YOU WITH THE ISSUE SO THAT THE SIGNALS TO THE BRAIN AND SUBSEQUENT RELIEF FELT IS GOING TO BE MORE NOTICEABLE.

Then, take a moment to rate how intense or bad that emotion or pain is. I use a compact Subjective Units of Distress Scale (SUDS) of 0–10, where 0 marks feeling neutral or good, and 10 marks intense discomfort. However, if you are in the heat of the moment and you are feeling sad, panicked or in pain, just start tapping on the top of your head and work through the points.

The purpose of tuning in is to connect you with the issue so that the signals to the brain and subsequent relief felt is going to be more noticeable. If you are tuned in and feeling an 8–10 on the scale, then you are going to notice a reduction in stress and discomfort quickly. Having the benchmark using this scale is also useful when you start using tapping to help you notice the difference in how you feel. Not everyone's energy shifts are the same; some people cry, yawn or even burp, so the scale is to help you notice your own improvement and shift in energy. After a while, you won't need to use the scale because you will intuitively know when you're feeling better.

2. Create Your Set-up Statement

Now you have given some thought to how you feel, what is bothering you and where in your body you feel it, you can use this information to create your set-up statement. It might help to write this down before you start tapping, especially if you are new to the technique.

You can use the following formula for your set-up statement:

'Even though I have this
[insert colour]
[insert emotion]
[insert location]
I choose to forgive, love and accept myself anyway.'

For example: Even though I have this red anger in my throat, I choose to forgive, love and accept myself anyway.

If you know why you are feeling this way, you can add that in, too.

Once you have your clear statement, close your eyes, take three deep breaths and tap continuously on the side of your hand while you say your statement one to three times. You can say the words out loud (or in your head), and you can vary what you say each time.

Here's an example of how one statement may change:

1. Even though I've got all of this heavy **blue anxiety and fear in my chest** because I have to present to the whole company tomorrow, I choose to forgive, love and accept myself anyway.
2. Even though I'm feeling so much **blue anxiety and fear in my chest** because I don't like presenting, I choose to forgive, love and accept myself anyway.
3. Even though I'm feeling so much **blue anxiety and fear** because I'm scared I'm going to mess up this presentation and everyone will see me fail, I choose to forgive, love and accept myself anyway.

3. Tap the Points Using Your Reminder Statement

Create a reminder statement that is a short summary of how you feel. For example, 'Blue anxiety and fear in my chest'.

Once you have your reminder statement, tap the points in sequence, starting at the top of the head. For the first one or two rounds of tapping (each a full sequence of points), really focus on the negative emotion you are feeling.

Repeat the reminder statement, or parts of it, for the first few tapping points. Then, when you feel ready, you can state the cause of the emotion. Sometimes it helps to visualize talking to a therapist or friend about the situation while you talk and tap. Don't overthink this; allow the words on how you feel about the situation to just flow while you tap.

As your body begins to relax a little, you can move into more neutral territory where you start to look at the situation from a different perspective, or with hindsight if you are thinking about something from the past. These neutral statements might be, 'Maybe it's okay that I feel this way?' or, 'Maybe this isn't about me and they were just having a bad day?'

You can then progress to consciously and actively deciding to let go, which can also lead you into more positive territory, including the use of affirmations such as, 'I choose to let all this anxiety go' or, 'I'm releasing all this anxiety'.

See pages 44–5 for an example of this in practice.

4. Check In and Keep Tapping

It's useful to stop every one or two rounds and see how you are feeling. How would you rate it now on a SUDS scale of 0–10? Has it gone down or up? Take a moment to notice this and continue to tap.

When it comes to tapping, there is no perfect goal. It is not realistic to get down to 0 every time you tap. In some instances, tapping from a 10 to an 8 might make a massive difference, and maybe that's all the time you have available to you. If that's the case, great. You can always come back to it and go again later.

The act of reflecting gives you an opportunity to connect with your body. Any shift in your body is a good sign that the energy is moving and dissipating. Ask yourself, 'Is the energy reducing or intensifying?', 'Is it moving around my body?' and 'Has the colour or weight changed?' For example, the energy might move to your throat, turn red and feel like a block, and the emotion you might feel here is restricted. In this case, create a new set-up statement and reminder phrase, focusing on this new red block in your throat while you tap the points. Keep assessing your energy until you feel lighter and pain-free.

There is a tapping sequence template available to you on my website www.tappingwithsarahtobin.com, so you can download it and start writing your own words that are more specific to your life.

What to Do if Memories Surface

While working with this book, it is very likely that memories will start to surface. This is happening because your body and mind feel safe enough for the memory to become conscious, and find some sort of resolution. This is a wonderful sign that you are shifting energy in your body.

Gather a journal and a pen, and follow these steps when memories surface:

1

Breathe

Take a few deep breaths and allow yourself to start to feel calm. Keep your eyes open during the steps that follow.

2

Acknowledge

Witness this memory without judgement. Look at it with curiosity and think or say, 'Oh, it is interesting that this memory has resurfaced. I wonder what I need to let go of'.

3

Tune in and feel

Tune in to how you felt in that memory, or how you feel now thinking about that memory. Remind yourself that you are creating space and cultivating compassion to feel to support a release.

4

Start tapping

Tap on the top of your head and tap down through the points, focusing on the words, 'I am safe'. Continue deep breathing, keeping your eyes open.

5

Ground

Remind yourself of where you are and use your senses to take in your surroundings. What do you see, hear, smell, touch and sense? Journal on what came up for you to come back to later.

6

Seek support

If something has come up that is very traumatic or you feel requires help to reframe this experience and let it go, please reach out to an EFT practitioner.

Empowering Change

Let's practise tapping with a sequence to help you with the first step on this journey: taking responsibility for the change needed in your life. It may feel strange to start a book about processing trauma with an exercise on taking responsibility. But rest assured: this is about empowering yourself in preparation for transformation and actively choosing to make yourself part of the solution.

Experiencing trauma can leave us with feelings of guilt, shame and blame (see more in Chapter 9), which is a hard energy to move on from and keeps us stuck in a victim mindset. None of this is our fault. We are not taught how powerful our subconscious is and how negative thoughts can spiral and create a new reality, as we explored in Chapter 2. Life teaches us that we are powerless, and so we give so much of our power away to others as a result of this belief.

Instead, I encourage you to take radical responsibility. This is a choice to embrace ownership of our circumstances, not as a 'should' or a burden, but rather as a pathway to self-empowerment and personal freedom. When we approach mistakes, adversity and challenging periods with radical responsibility, we are not just accepting what has happened, we're choosing how we respond. Doing this is about being able to justify your own thoughts, rationale, behaviours and actions, and acknowledging that you have the power to create change in your life.

YOU HAVE THE POWER TO CREATE CHANGE IN YOUR LIFE.

It's Safe to Change

Often, before I've guided clients with the tools I use, I first lead them in some tapping to encourage the body to soften to change. Safety is a huge part of change, and the reason strategies are in place is because of the fear or feeling of being unsafe. If the ego doesn't feel safe to change, it is not going to allow change. It will resist the work you want to do.

It is widely considered that the subconscious mind has 95 per cent of the operating power and the conscious mind has 5 per cent. Therefore, we have to get into the subconscious mind for real change to happen. Expecting growth by working in the conscious mind alone is akin to walking up Mount Everest with no shoes on. It would be extremely difficult and require a huge amount of conscious effort.

The combination of tapping while talking about how we are feeling sends safety signals straight to the subconscious, which is a major benefit of tapping. Bringing safety into the mind, body and soul will support a healthy environment of release and reprogramming that will make a difference on this journey. The tapping sequence on pages 44–5 will help do this.

Tapping to Embrace Change

The following tapping sequence will help you to accept responsibility for your thoughts, emotions and actions. This will allow you to refocus on yourself, reclaim your power, release 'victim' energy (see page 42) and help your body feel safe to change.

Before doing this exercise, take a few minutes to connect with the energy of change. Does that cause you anxiety or fear? Notice any pains or tension in particular areas. Tune in, find the emotion, give it a colour and location, and rate the intensity from 0–10. Then, take three deep breaths, and follow the set-up steps below, inserting your own wording where this feels right:

SET-UP STATEMENT (TAPPING ON THE SIDE OF THE HAND):

Even though I feel black, heavy fear in my shoulders, I choose to forgive, love and accept myself anyway.

Even though I feel sad in my heart that I've given my power away and neglected my true self, I choose to forgive, love and accept myself anyway.

Even though it feels scary to change because I like to be in control of everything, I'm afraid of the unknown and afraid of who I really am, I choose to forgive, love and accept myself anyway.

Embracing Change Tapping Sequence

Commence tapping, starting at the top of the head and going down the points:

ToH: This dark, heavy fear in my shoulders

EB: This weight of heavy emotions

SoE: That I've held for so long now

UE: I've been feeling so stuck

UN: I've been holding myself back

CH: I have a lot of things to let go of

CB: I have experienced a lot of pain

UA: This pain manifests as negative thoughts, emotions and actions

IW: My body hasn't felt safe

TH: It hasn't felt safe for me to let go

FF: It hasn't felt safe to heal

MF: It hasn't felt safe to change

RF: It hasn't felt safe to grow

BF: It feels safer to stay where I am

ToH: It's stopped me doing the deeper work
EB: Maybe I am afraid of facing my pain
SoE: Maybe I am afraid I can't cope
UE: Or that I will never feel good again
UN: It feels so hard to take these steps
CH: This pending journey of discovery feels hard
CB: All this resistance in my body to change
UA: This is only the energy of fear trying to keep me safe
IW: I recognize what this is and I choose to let it go
TH: I am ready now to rebalance and realign myself
FF: I am ready to let go of the responsibility of others
MF: I am ready to claim responsibility for myself
RF: I am ready to make a change
BF: I am ready to find my true self again

ToH: Perhaps I have felt the victim
EB: I felt so powerless for so long
SoE: Because so many things that have happened in my life have hurt me
UE: So many things out of my control
UN: I've been focusing on pleasing others
CH: I've felt responsible for their happiness
CB: In the process, I've forgotten myself
UA: I've not been taking responsibility for myself
IW: I didn't realize this was happening
TH: It wasn't my fault
FF: I didn't know any better
MF: I was just doing what I thought was best
RF: It was best for me at that time
BF: My ego stepped in to keep me safe and that's okay

ToH: I choose now to release all my fear of change
EB: I let go of any victim energy that is holding me back
SoE: I can take responsibility for myself now
UE: I choose to let go and heal
UN: I choose to remember my soul's power
CH: I know change is necessary and possible
CB: I know change is going to be great for me
UA: I know I am ready for change
IW: I am so excited by the change that is coming into my life
TH: I choose to feel safe in my body
FF: I know it's safe to change
MF: I choose to accept and forgive
RF: I choose to be my authentic self
BF: I choose to love all parts of myself

CHECK-IN

How are you feeling now? Rate yourself on a scale of 0–10. What number are you? Has the intensity dropped? Does your body feel any lighter? Did any memories surface? Feel free to repeat the exercise.

STEP 2:
PEELING BACK THE LAYERS

In this step, we will go deeper into understanding ourselves, acknowledging the complex emotions and experiences that shape our journey. This step invites you to explore the emotions you may have suppressed or overlooked, offering tools to ground yourself in the present and stay connected to your inner resilience. You'll be guided on how to develop greater compassion for yourself through the healing act of forgiveness. Through tapping, you'll learn how to manage overwhelm, burnout and the impact of unresolved grief or trauma. You'll be supported along the way, building your confidence in your own empowered ability to heal.

CHAPTER 4

Tapping into Your Emotions

Emotions are signals and feedback from our inner world, moving through us to reveal any unmet needs or imbalances.

Emotion

The word emotion is often said to be 'energy in motion'. It is also linked to the Latin verb *emovere*, meaning 'to move away, remove, or dislodge'.

'I'm sad' in the Irish language is 'tá brón orm', which means 'sadness is on me'. This is a lovely reminder that we are not our emotions. We are not an angry person. Anger doesn't own us. We are feeling anger as a transient expression of this current moment.

Most of us can feel disturbance in our energy system. On a simple level, it can feel either good or bad. For example, when we are out with friends and everyone is happy, laughing and smiling, we may feel joy and gratitude. However, when we visit a relative in hospital or a nursing home, we may feel sad, anxious and uncertain.

What Are Emotions?

Emotions are signals and feedback from our inner world, moving through us to reveal any unmet needs or imbalances. They help you make meaning of your life, and tell you something about an environment, person or yourself.

Your energy field is constantly scanning every situation, looking for safety and a sense of belonging. If the body senses danger, there is a chemical reaction as it switches into the sympathetic nervous system and the body is flooded with cortisol and adrenaline. If the body senses safety, it'll stay in its existing state of relative calm and balance, or other chemicals such as endorphins may be produced.

Not only is the physiology of your blood changing constantly, but also emotions often inform you react to your environment. There is a complex dance that happens between our thoughts and emotions. Some believe the emotion comes first, which then informs thoughts and actions, and others believe thoughts come first, which inform what we feel. Regardless of the debate on which comes first, they are both intrinsically linked, and perhaps work closely together in a clever feedback loop system.

Stuck Emotions

What we might think of as stuck or trapped emotions are actually unprocessed emotions. This is when emotions are suppressed, where we consciously try to avoid thinking about or talking about how we feel; or when emotions are repressed, where we unconsciously block unwanted thoughts or impulses. Linking back to energy, if we are avoiding how we are feeling, we are not processing the energy we have generated. Where does it go and what impact does it have?

Researchers call this 'embodied emotion',[1] where feelings are consciously or unconsciously felt in the body. The physical body houses the energy that isn't released. It can be stored in many places, but studies have found the energy is mostly connected with the heart, lungs and stomach.

Dr Bessel van der Kolk, a renowned psychiatrist and trauma specialist who wrote the book *The Body Keeps The Score,* explains that trauma is stored in the body. He believes the body remembers the trauma and associated emotions, even if the conscious mind has long forgotten, and this remaining energy manifests as physical ailments and psychosomatic conditions.

Emotions are connected to the formation of beliefs because the brain is wired to create meaning from experience. Repeated negative emotions will cause our brains to create a belief that both explains and predicts future experiences. But evidence suggests that if we process and release our emotions they won't be stored in the body, and they will have less impact on us physically, emotionally and mentally.

Disconnection

When on a healing journey, it is important to start paying attention to our emotions, because not understanding how our emotions shape our thoughts and decisions allows us to become disembodied and disconnected.

Disconnection comes from an unconscious survival tactic created early in life to protect ourselves. This detachment from our emotions is often called 'jumping ship', leaving us feeling that a part of our soul has left our body.

When we are disconnected, we lose awareness of our feelings and the subsequent understanding they bring. That disconnection can lead to conscious and unconscious distraction and misinterpretation of situations. Fear and excitement can often feel the same in the body. For someone who has experienced a lot of fear in the past, when they feel excited, they misinterpret the feeling of excitement and in turn start to feel anxious about upcoming events. In childhood, we may be told to be quiet or feel unheard, and we can interpret this as signifying that our emotions are invalid and unsafe to express. We may then suppress them, lock them away and forget they are signals and something useful to be acted upon.

Trauma brings a heightened state of stress and emotions, which can enhance disconnection. Even after the event we may still feel the residue of 'freeze' (see page 30), which manifests as procrastination. Emotional detachment is often the best and only strategy during difficult times, but the long-term impact can be damaging when finding a partner, becoming a parent or navigating stressful work situations, hindering our ability to thrive.

Connection

Reconnecting with our emotions is important for our long-term health, because feeling them, acknowledging them and giving them a voice is part of the process of letting them go. For someone who has been disconnected for a while, even the thought of reconnecting can feel overwhelming. But here are a few practical ways to get started:

Check in
Start a daily practice of asking yourself: how am I? Listen for a response in your body or mind.

Mindful moments or meditation
Take some time regularly to quieten your world. Find somewhere free of distractions and allow yourself to be present and notice how your body feels.

Body scan
Close your eyes and mentally scan your body from head to toe, focusing on one area at a time. Notice sensations such as warmth, tightness or pain without judgement, and breathe into any areas of discomfort to deepen your mind-body connection.

Move your body
Use gentle movement to shift your energy. Notice how your body feels after different types of movement and repeat the types that make you shift your energy and feel good.

Common Emotions

To connect with your authentic self, it's good to understand your emotions and what they mean. Here are some key emotions explained:

Grief is a process that includes multiple emotions that are connected to loss, longing or feeling lost. Grief is often described as a journey of learning to live with loss.

Anxiety arises from feeling a loss of control or facing uncertainty. It is often coupled with worried and repetitive thoughts, and hypervigilance to any potential dangers.

Sadness is a response to loss or defeat, often felt in the heart or chest area. It signals that something isn't right and might need to change.

Overwhelm is an extreme level of stress where we struggle to function. Clarity and rational thinking are reduced, and our critical voice may increase.

Shame is linked to our sense of self. Unlike guilt, it says 'I am bad', rather than 'I've done a bad thing'. Shame challenges our worth and values, which can feel very uncomfortable.

Stress is when we feel like we can't cope in our current situation, leading to tension and the release of our stress hormones. The root of this reaction often comes from the belief that we aren't good enough.

Guilt is when we feel bad about something we've done, often accompanied by regret. This is linked to our specific behaviours and can prompt us to repair.

Fear is a response to immediate threat or danger, like a fear of flying. It can be linked to physical danger or a threat to one's sense of self.

Tapping for Anxiety

Anxiety is such a common emotion that is easily identified. It can be felt in the body in different ways; for example when we feel nervous or tense or experience shallow breathing, panic and a quickening heart rate. It can feel like walking on eggshells, waiting for the next difficult situation to present itself. Rumination, negative thoughts and doubts can also surface.

Before doing this exercise, take a few minutes to connect with the energy of anxiety and find it in your body. Call to mind the situation that you are feeling anxious about, or think about a situation that has you on edge. This is an ideal tapping sequence to use when panic starts to build. If you don't feel anxious right now, you can recall a time in the past and use that memory to invoke anxiety.

Tune in, find the emotion, give it a colour and location, and rate the intensity from 0–10. Then, take three deep breaths, and follow the set-up steps and sequence, inserting your own wording where this feels right:

SET-UP STATEMENT (TAPPING ON THE SIDE OF THE HAND):

Even though I have this yellow anxiety in my stomach, I choose to forgive, love and accept myself anyway.

Even though I feel yellow anxiety in my stomach because I'm so worried, I choose to forgive, love and accept myself anyway.

Even though I feel so worried, and my stomach is nervous with this yellow anxiety, I choose to allow myself to start feeling calm.

Anxiety Tapping Sequence

Commence tapping, starting at the top of the head and going down the points:

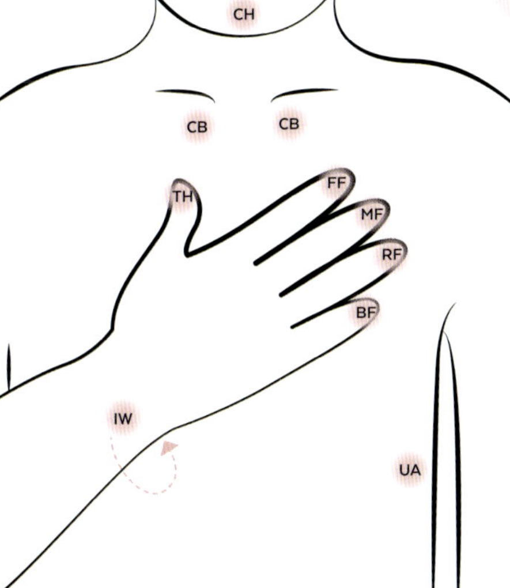

ToH: This yellow anxiety in my stomach

EB: All this yellow anxiety

SoE: I feel so nervous in my stomach

UE: I'm full of worry

UN: I can't stop thinking of this situation

CH: It's making me feel so anxious

CB: All this anxiety in my stomach

UA: It's causing me to panic

IW: This panic in my body

TH: Is starting to build

FF: This tension feels so uncomfortable

MF: I don't feel safe

RF: This worry and anxiety in my stomach

BF: I hate feeling all this stress

ToH: I keep worrying about this situation/the future
EB: I keep worrying about certain things happening
SoE: My mind is full of 'what ifs'
UE: It's making me feel so stressed in my stomach
UN: I worry I won't be able to cope
CH: I'm thinking of different scenarios and outcomes
CB: I'm struggling to stay present
UA: With all this worry of the future
IW: Things feel so uncertain
TH: I hate uncertainty
FF: I don't like feeling out of control
MF: I love to feel in control
RF: Right now, I feel out of control
BF: And that's causing this yellow anxiety in my stomach

ToH: Maybe my thoughts are causing all this anxiety
EB: Maybe some of these scenarios will happen
SoE: Maybe none of these scenarios will happen
UE: Maybe my mind has run away with me
UN: Maybe I'm overthinking things
CH: Maybe I don't have to worry so much
CB: Maybe I can't control everything
UA: Even though I want to control everything
IW: Maybe there are some things I can't control
TH: Maybe it's okay to not always be in control
FF: Maybe I can cope with whatever happens
MF: Maybe I don't have to worry so much
RF: Maybe I can let go of this anxiety
BF: What would it feel like to let go of this worry?

ToH: I choose now to let go of this anxiety
EB: I choose to dissolve this yellow anxiety in my stomach
SoE: I choose to let go of the need to control
UE: I choose to relax a little
UN: I choose to trust myself a little more
CH: I choose to believe I can cope
CB: I choose to believe in myself more
UA: I let go of all this tension in my body
IW: I allow my mind to let go
TH: I release the tight grip of control
FF: I choose to bring peace into my body
MF: I lean into the energy of peace and love
RF: I feel full compassion for myself
BF: I choose to love myself completely

CHECK-IN
How are you feeling now? Rate yourself on a scale of 0–10. What number are you? Has the intensity dropped? Does your body feel any lighter? Did any memories surface? Feel free to repeat the exercise.

CHAPTER 5

Tapping for Grounding

Grounding is a powerful return to presence.

Grounding

What is your default state of being? Are you running around, always busy with a million to-do lists, and overwhelmed? Or worried about the future and ruminating on the past? We can probably assume that in this modern world, a lot of us are being governed by the mind. We are distracted, anxious and often disconnected from our bodies. We are living in autopilot without conscious intention.

GROUNDING IS A WAY OF BRINGING YOURSELF MINDFULLY INTO THE CURRENT MOMENT.

The antidote to this way of life is grounding: the act of being aware of our bodies and our environment. Grounding is a powerful return to presence. It is a way of bringing yourself mindfully into the current moment, often linked to the act of placing your bare skin on the earth and connecting yourself with Earth's frequencies. Grounding works by creating an electric charge that flows into your body when you are in direct contact with earth. These positive electrons neutralize positively charged free radicals and restore balance. Being grounded allows you to be mentally and emotionally stable.

The Benefits of Grounding

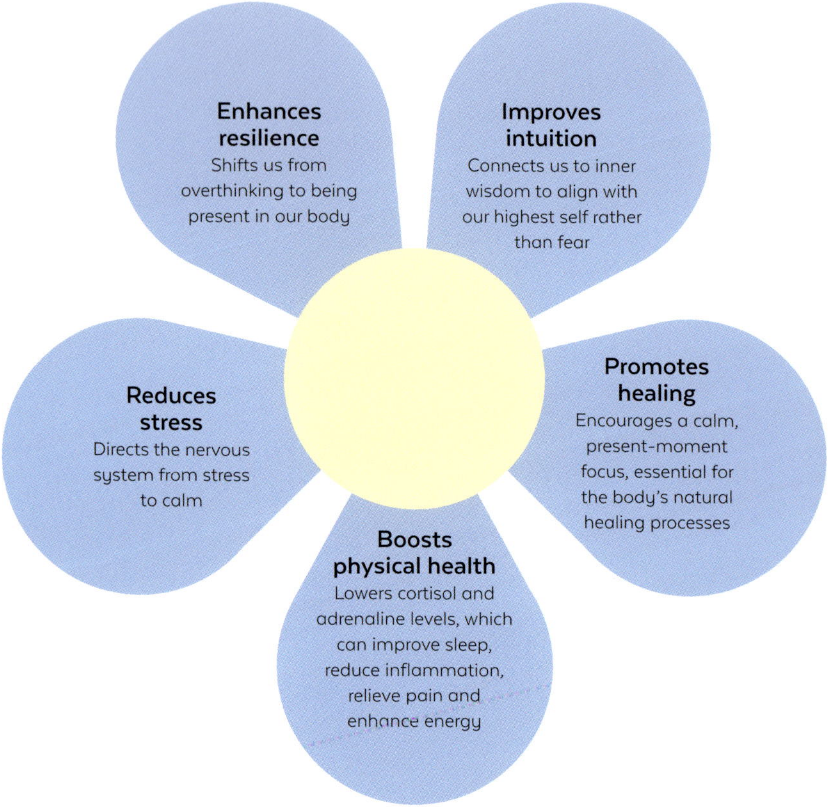

Enhances resilience
Shifts us from overthinking to being present in our body

Improves intuition
Connects us to inner wisdom to align with our highest self rather than fear

Reduces stress
Directs the nervous system from stress to calm

Promotes healing
Encourages a calm, present-moment focus, essential for the body's natural healing processes

Boosts physical health
Lowers cortisol and adrenaline levels, which can improve sleep, reduce inflammation, relieve pain and enhance energy

Ways to Ground Yourself

Nature

One of the quickest, easiest and cheapest ways to ground yourself is to get out into nature. Being outdoors and embracing the natural and powerful healing properties of the Sun also improves our circadian rhythms, so if you can access nature in the sunshine, you'll benefit greatly.

1. Try taking a stroll in your favourite place with focused intention. You might like to walk barefoot in a field, lay down on the grass in the sunshine or use your hand to take droplets of dew off a morning rose.
2. Whatever you choose to do, ask yourself: what can I hear? What sounds are far away? What sounds are close by? What can I see? What can I smell? What can I touch along the way?
3. Look closely at your surroundings, starting at your feet and the ground, moving to the foreground, the middle ground and background. Look at them as though you are going to recreate the scene in a future painting.

Visualizing

This technique can be useful for people who have reduced mobility and for those who can't access nature as much as they would like.

1. Lie down on a bed or on the floor, or sit in a comfortable position.
2. Imagine a pillar of white and gold light coming down from the sky and entering your whole body. See the pillar of light flowing through you all the way down into the earth so your body is the anchor point or bridge between heaven and Earth.
3. From the base of your spine or the soles of your feet, imagine roots that grow down into the earth through all the layers of soil, rock, crystals, caves and waters, right through to the Earth's core.
4. At the core, imagine a huge crystal of your choice and wrap your roots around the crystal.
5. Gratefully acknowledge the Earth's healing energy and welcome the energy back up through your roots and into your body and energy field.
6. Finish by imagining a protective layer around this bubble, shielding you from anything that does not serve your highest self.

Plant Medicine

Plants are part of nature and you can use them in a variety of ways to bring the frequency of the Earth into your body.

You can smell essential oils or take flower and plant essences, but if you are called to go deeper and to work with plant medicine, please seek support from a professional practitioner.

Essential Oils

Essential oils are the natural oils and liquids produced by plants and flowers. They can calm the autonomic nervous system using the vagus nerve and sending signals of safety to the body, reducing stress and anxiety. You can hold a bottle of essential oil under your nose and breathe deeply, add drops to your bath or diffuser or even create your own roller bottle by diluting your favourite essential in a carrier oil like fractionated coconut oil.

Here are some oils you can smell to calm and soothe your nervous system, allowing you to come back into the present moment:

- Bergamot
- Cedarwood
- Clary sage
- Frankincense
- Lavender
- Neroli
- Patchouli
- Rose
- Sandalwood
- Vetiver

Flower and Plant Essences

Similarly to essential oils, flower essences are a distillation of plant liquids, but they are processed differently so that they are safe to ingest and take orally. Essences are taken via a dropper by delivering a few drops under the tongue or adding to water to sip during the day. The oils and essences encourage the body to heal itself by raising the frequency of the body.

Here are some essences that can be used to aid a calming and grounded sensation within the body and energy field:

- Ivy encourages grounded energy despite the chaos surrounding you.
- Star of Bethlehem releases current and stored shock from the body, allowing for more presence.
- Mediterranean sage encourages the qualities of warmth, comfort and quiet wisdom.
- Dandelion connects you to your authentic self and keeps you focused.
- Carrot can help you get organized and move forward with decisions, and also aids creativity.
- Clematis for daydreamers helps to bring focus to take those dreams into aligned action.

Crystals

Crystals are gifted from Mother Earth, and people across the world use them every day to help themselves stay grounded. Each crystal has a high frequency, which when worn or connected with can improve our own frequency. These are my favourite crystals for keeping me grounded and present:

- Clear quartz helps to connect to Earth's essence and brings clarity and focus.
- Smokey quartz helps to remove unwanted negative energies, move on from the past and connect more with the present moment.
- Selenite wands are excellent for cleansing negative energy, providing clarity and fostering a sense of calm.

There are also plenty of books on crystals you can explore such as *The Crystal Bible* series by Judy Hall and *The Crystal Apothecary* by Gemma Petherbridge.

Solfeggio frequencies

These are specific tones of sound that are reputed to raise and improve the frequency of your body, bring your body back to balance, aid healing and have been found to improve PTSD, anxiety and physical illness. These specific tones are said to date back to ancient chants and sounds used in Western Christianity and Eastern Indian religions. Dr Joseph Puleo rediscovered them[1] in the 1970s, making them popular again over time.

You can search for these specific frequencies online and pick which frequency resonates with you in any moment. These frequencies are said to improve sleep significantly and can be used for the whole family to bring grounded energy into the home.

Opposite are some different frequencies and their benefits:[2]

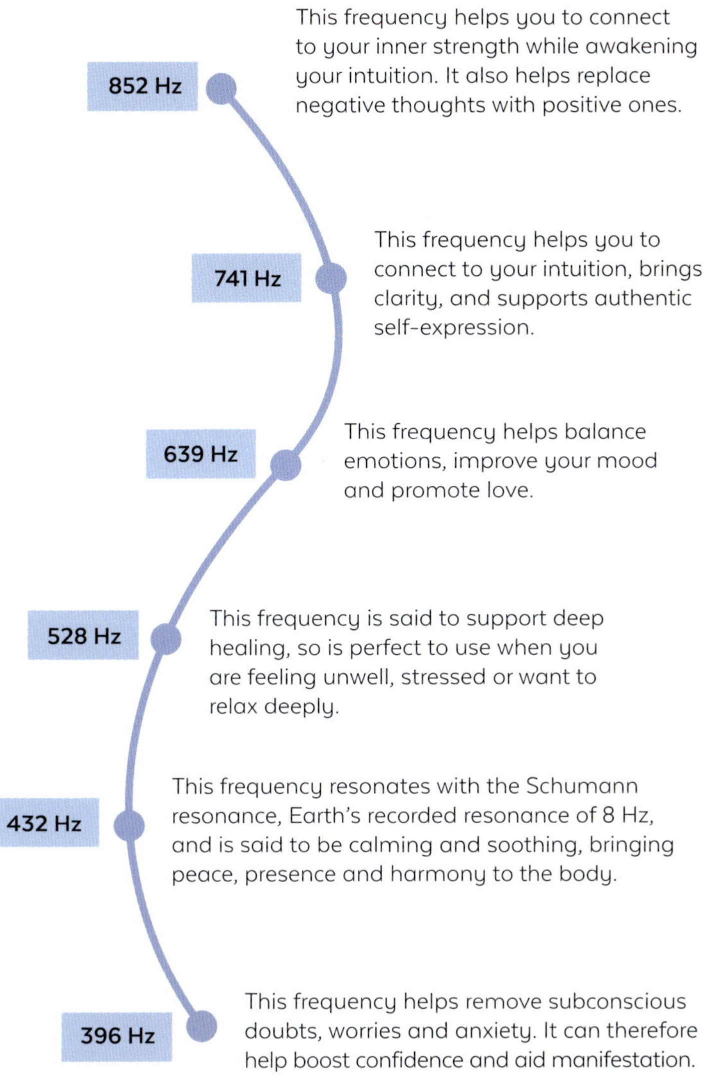

852 Hz

This frequency helps you to connect to your inner strength while awakening your intuition. It also helps replace negative thoughts with positive ones.

741 Hz

This frequency helps you to connect to your intuition, brings clarity, and supports authentic self-expression.

639 Hz

This frequency helps balance emotions, improve your mood and promote love.

528 Hz

This frequency is said to support deep healing, so is perfect to use when you are feeling unwell, stressed or want to relax deeply.

432 Hz

This frequency resonates with the Schumann resonance, Earth's recorded resonance of 8 Hz, and is said to be calming and soothing, bringing peace, presence and harmony to the body.

396 Hz

This frequency helps remove subconscious doubts, worries and anxiety. It can therefore help boost confidence and aid manifestation.

Tapping for Grounding

Tapping switches off the stress response, aligns us with feelings of safety and allows the body and mind to come back into the present moment. It is an effective stand-alone tool or can be used in conjunction with the other methods of grounding shared in this chapter. You can use this tapping sequence anytime, anywhere to remind yourself that you are safe and present.

Before doing this exercise, take a few minutes to connect with yourself and see how busy your mind is. What is happening in your life that is distracting you or making you predict the future? What area of your life is causing you the most stress? Notice any pains or tension in particular areas.

Tune in, find the emotion, give it a colour and location, and rate the intensity from 0–10. Then, take three deep breaths, and follow the set-up steps and sequence, inserting your own wording where this feels right:

SET-UP STATEMENT (TAPPING ON THE SIDE OF THE HAND):

Even though I feel black, heavy stress in my head and it doesn't feel safe to be fully present in this moment, I choose to forgive, love and accept myself anyway.

Even though I am feeling numb and disconnected from my body because I've got so much going on, I choose to forgive, love and accept myself anyway.

Even though it doesn't feel safe to be fully present in my body right now and something has me feeling unsafe, I choose to allow myself to start feeling safe.

Grounding Tapping Sequence

Commence tapping, starting at the top of the head and going down the points:

ToH: This black, heavy stress in my head

EB: I'm so caught up in my head

SoE: I'm so disconnected with my body

UE: I can't even identify how I am feeling right now

UN: I feel numb

CH: Yet my mind is whirling

CB: So many thoughts

UA: So many things to be doing

IW: I am thinking of all the things I need to do

TH: Yet I'm also reminded of times in the past

FF: I feel stressed and overwhelmed

MF: I am not fully present right now

RF: I am struggling to pay full attention to things

BF: I'm totally distracted

ToH
EB
SoE
UE
UN
CH
CB
CB
FF
TH
MF
RF
BF
IW
UA

ToH: I can't fully connect with my body
EB: I sometimes feel numb
SoE: I feel my mind and spirit are somewhere else
UE: I feel so disconnected
UN: Like I've 'jumped ship'
CH: I don't feel safe in my body right now
CB: Because I am thinking too much about the past
UA: And am worried for the future
IW: I've been through so much already
TH: I've been through difficult times
FF: I've experienced a lot of pain
MF: Which has made me disconnect from my body
RF: I struggle to connect to the real me
BF: Sometimes it doesn't feel safe to be my authentic self

ToH: This may have happened a long time ago
EB: Maybe it felt safe to disconnect at that time
SoE: Maybe I haven't fully come back into my body
UE: Maybe I didn't feel safe in my past
UN: Maybe lots of different things made me feel scared
CH: Maybe I can feel safe in this present moment
CB: Maybe I can bring safety into my body
UA: Maybe I don't have to hold onto all this pain and fear
IW: Maybe I can connect with my authentic self again
TH: Maybe I can open myself up to my emotions
FF: Maybe I can dissolve the numbness in my body
MF: Maybe I can feel safe AND feel my emotions at the same time
RF: Emotions are just energy and it's safe to feel energy
BF: It's also safe to let all this energy go

ToH: I choose to let go of all this overwhelm in my head
EB: I choose to let go of feeling unsafe and anxious
SoE: I acknowledge all that happened in the past
UE: I choose to understand that it is not happening now
UN: I choose to bring safety into my body
CH: I let go of the feeling that I'm in danger
CB: I am very safe right now
UA: I allow my body to relax and feel safe
IW: It's safe to feel safe
TH: I welcome all my energy home into this present moment
FF: I allow myself to be here in this moment
MF: I allow myself to feel grounded
RF: It's time now to feel safe
BF: I am safe and here in this precious moment

CHECK-IN

How are you feeling now? Rate yourself on a scale of 0–10. What number are you? Has the intensity dropped? Does your body feel any lighter? Did any memories surface? Feel free to repeat the exercise.

CHAPTER 6

Tapping for Overwhelm and Burnout

By recognizing the signs of overwhelm and using tools like tapping, we can release pressure, resist burnout, reclaim trust in ourselves and restore balance.

Perfectly Imperfect

Many of us learn that when we behave a certain way, we get positive attention and feel loved. Did you get in trouble as a child if you got your clothes dirty? Did you lie and try your best to cover up your mistakes or accidents? Did you have to act a certain way to please the people around you? This is conditional love; when we fulfil an expectation or condition, we receive affection and attention. But this kind of reinforcement can often lead to fawning (see page 30) behaviours in adulthood.

Wanting things to be perfect is understandable; it's a safety strategy. However, this pressure adds a huge amount of workload to our already full lives and never-ending to-do lists, and can contribute to feelings of overwhelm and burnout. On an extreme scale, it can be very limiting, exhausting and controlling.

If we release our grasp on the need to be perfect and the need for external validation, then we can release some of that internal pressure. It will then have a knock-on impact on our overwhelm. Doing our best is good enough and remember, no one is perfect. We are all perfectly imperfect and imperfectly perfect.

DOING OUR BEST IS GOOD ENOUGH AND REMEMBER, NO ONE IS PERFECT.

Overwhelm and Burnout

Sometimes the pressure to be perfect gets the better of us and we try to take on more than we can handle. In this state, all we can think about is the endless to-do list, the places to be and the hustle and bustle of managing our lives. This leaves us feeling a huge amount of pressure, whether it's coming from others or ourselves.

We might feel exhausted and deflated after a stressful time, but usually our overwhelm is short-lived if we get some time to rest, get on top of our list, get help or reaffirm our boundaries. It is very easy to write off short periods of overwhelm as a bad month or a challenging time. However, if these tough times persist, we may start to allow stress and tension to feel normal. At this point, chronic stress can set in because our cortisol and adrenaline levels rise and stay high, causing our threshold or window of tolerance to decrease (see page 30).

When overwhelm persists, our bodies start to respond to perceived threats with a heightened sense of anxiety that makes rational thinking difficult. This is because our body cells are constantly in fight, flight, freeze or fawn (see page 30), without enough rest. They are exhausted, overloaded with toxins and not regenerating properly, which can lead to a myriad of physical, emotional and mental issues.

Over time, this state can evolve into burnout: a chronic, consuming fatigue that saps joy, resilience, motivation and our sense of self. In burnout, there is no let up. Stress feels all encompassing, never-ending and hopeless. Fatigue takes over, sleep is poor, it's hard to maintain a healthy diet and we might even partake in some numbing activities such as drinking more alcohol than usual.

Unfortunately, burnout creeps up on us often without big warning signs. It is a deeper and more prolonged state of emotional, physical and mental exhaustion. It is when overwhelm becomes an intense and permanent state. It is chronic yet over time it becomes our normal. We can't remember what life feels like when we are calm, present and happy.

Overwhelm is a precursor to burnout so it is important to keep on top of managing this tension in your body and your mindset. By recognizing the signs of overwhelm and using tools like tapping, we can release pressure, resist burnout, reclaim trust in ourselves and restore balance. Looking after your physical health is also extremely important to avoid strain on areas such as your adrenal glands. Please make sure you are seeking professional advice so you know what to do to build yourself back up physically alongside the emotional and mental support you receive.

Overwhelm and Self-sabotage

Feeling overwhelmed can make us think we can't cope. Our body is tired, our mind is frazzled and we don't feel able to handle present challenges. This feeling and belief might hold us back from pursuing our dreams because we don't trust in our ability to succeed.

But what if overwhelm is not a sign of inability? What if it's our ego's strategy to keep us safe in our comfort zone? Sometimes, overwhelm is our mind's sneaky attempt at self-sabotage, creating resistance to change at a time when courage from within is needed the most to push ourselves forward.

As discussed previously in this chapter, when overwhelm is genuine (and not a sabotaging safety strategy), it builds over time into a load so heavy and suffocating that we lose touch with reality and our true authentic selves. Self-awareness is key here to identify whether we need genuine rest and recovery, or support with our mindset and emotional barriers to break free of our comfort zone and reach our next level.

Am I self-sabotaging or burned out?

Try this quiz to help you identify whether you are self-sabotaging or genuinely burned out. You may also relate to both answers, indicating that you are feeling the impact of both burnout and long-term limiting beliefs and self-sabotage. Feel free to journal on these questions before or after the quiz for deeper self-exploration and reflection.

Start here:

1. Am I sleeping and eating well?

Yes Go to question 2

No Burnout alert! Your body might need more rest and nourishment.

2. When was the last time I felt relaxed, and tension- and pain-free?

Recently Go to question 3

Can't remember Burnout alert! Your body is asking for a break.

3. Have I got too much on my plate and can't keep up?

Yes Go to question 4

No Go to question 5

4. Have I asked for and accepted help with some of my tasks?

Yes Go to question 5

No Self-sabotage alert! Holding back on asking for help could be rooted in fear of letting go.

5. Have I shared how I'm feeling with others?

Yes Go to question 6

No Burnout alert! Sometimes, bottling things up can lead to isolation and exhaustion.

6. What am I most afraid of right now?

Failure or judgement Self-sabotage alert! Fear may be holding you back from being your true self and achieving your dreams.

Nothing specific Go to question 7

7. Am I pushing myself too hard, or am I scared of failure?

Pushing too hard Burnout alert! You may be overextending your limits.

Scared of failure Self-sabotage alert! Fear could be stopping you from reaching your full potential.

8. Have I felt this way only recently or for a long time?

Just recently Burnout alert! It might be time to rest, reflect and recharge.

For a long time Dual alert! Lingering feelings suggest burnout paired with deeper fears or beliefs holding you back. A dual approach – recharging while addressing patterns – could help you feel more balanced.

Tapping for Overwhelm and Burnout

Tapping supports us when we feel overwhelmed and burned out by switching off our stress response. This allows us to regulate our nervous system, reduce stress, increase our energy, feel calmer, regain clarity about the tasks at hand, lower a perfectionist mindset, stop people pleasing and address limiting beliefs. It can change our mindset and boost our confidence so we feel we can cope.

Before doing this exercise, take a few minutes to connect with the energy of overwhelm in your body. Have you been pushing yourself hard lately? Have you been giving your energy away to others? Have you been holding yourself back? Notice any pains or tension in particular areas.

Tune in, find the emotion, give it a colour and location, and rate the intensity from 0–10. Then, take three deep breaths, and follow the set-up steps and sequence, inserting your own wording where this feels right:

SET-UP STATEMENT (TAPPING ON THE SIDE OF THE HAND):

Even though I feel blue overwhelm in my neck and shoulders because I have so much going on and I feel exhausted, I choose to forgive, love and accept myself anyway.

Even though I have this heavy weight in my neck and shoulders because I'm so overwhelmed and don't think I can cope, I choose to forgive, love and accept myself anyway.

Even though I feel the heavy weight of depletion in every cell of my body, I choose to forgive, love and accept myself anyway.

Overwhelm and Burnout Tapping Sequence

Commence tapping, starting at the top of the head and going down the points:

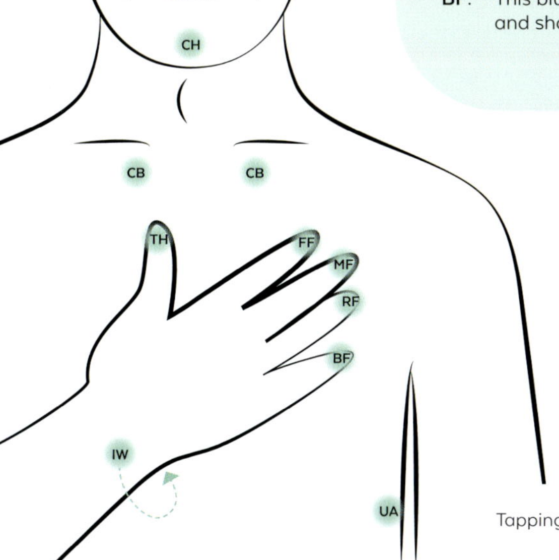

ToH: This blue overwhelm in my neck and shoulders

EB: This heavy blue weight

SoE: This overwhelm is weighing me down

UE: Everything feels so heavy

UN: I've so much on

CH: I feel totally depleted

CB: I feel exhausted

UA: I feel like I'm struggling

IW: I feel like I can't cope

TH: I've taken on so much

FF: So much pressure and burden

MF: I've so much to do

RF: Everything feels so hard

BF: This blue pressure in my neck and shoulders

ToH: Maybe I can release some of this pressure
EB: Maybe I can let go of this overwhelm
SoE: Maybe I have got what it takes
UE: Maybe I can cope
UN: Maybe I can get more support
CH: Maybe I can ease this pressure
CB: Maybe it doesn't need to be perfect
UA: Maybe done is good enough
IW: I choose to start releasing this overwhelm
TH: I choose to let go of this pressure
FF: I choose to nourish my mind, body and soul
MF: I give myself compassion
RF: I'm going through a lot
BF: I am doing the best I can

ToH: I am perfectly imperfect
EB: I am imperfectly perfect
SoE: I always try so hard
UE: Anything I give is enough
UN: I let go of the overwhelm I carry
CH: I know I am enough
CB: I can cope with life
UA: I am coping
IW: I can get through this experience
TH: Nothing is permanent
FF: I give myself permission to rest
MF: I allow myself to let go
RF: I am enough exactly as I am
BF: I am more than enough

ToH: I release all remaining overwhelm
EB: I release all stress from my body
SoE: I release all exhaustion
UE: I restore calm in my body
UN: I restore balance
CH: I choose to feel enough
CB: I choose to believe I can cope
UA: I choose to listen to my body
IW: And give it what it needs
TH: I am worthy of rest and nourishment
FF: I am worthy of support
MF: I have compassion for all parts of me
RF: I love all parts of me
BF: I am whole exactly as I am

CHECK-IN

How are you feeling now? Rate yourself on a scale of 0–10. What number are you? Has the intensity dropped? Does your body feel any lighter? Did any memories surface? Feel free to repeat the exercise.

CHAPTER 7

Tapping for Grief and PTSD

You can't erase grief; you just learn to live with it and, over time, it finds a place in your life.

Grief

Unfortunately, at some point in our lives, everyone will know grief. It is not a singular emotion but a kaleidoscope of different energies that accompany you on your journey. There may be sadness, anger, disappointment, denial, fear, anxiety and more.

Grief is non-linear and can come out of nowhere, giving you whiplash and reminding you it's there, before fading away into the shadows. It is mercurial - unpredictable in nature. Many say you can't erase grief; you just learn to live with it, and over time, it finds a place in your life.

Grief is what started me on this journey of self-discovery because I didn't want to live with the intense emotions that were keeping me frozen in time. The uncomfortable sensations and subsequent numbness were not the way I wanted to live for the rest of my life. At 33, I was not going to give up, and I made the conscious choice to find a path forward with grief that was less intense so that I could find happiness again.

The Nature of Grief

Grief can feel big and small. It can feel heavy and light. And it can exist alongside joy, contentment and love. For big traumatic events, our grief is very evident, prominent and obvious to others. In these situations, we often have people rallying around, offering support and encouraging proactive actions. But grief can also be created in comparatively less significant situations.

Sometimes we are unaware that we hold grief within us. Smaller, more regular traumas can often lead to even more damaging results as they impact the development of our belief system, especially when experienced in our early years. This grief might be less obvious to both us and others, and the impact may not be felt straight away. This can lead us to feel isolated in our pain and suffering.

The Roots of Grief

BRING COMPASSION TO YOUR THOUGHTS AND ACTIONS WHEN NAVIGATING LIFE WITH GRIEF IN YOUR SIDECAR.

Grief is primarily caused by loss. This could be the loss of an important person in our lives; the loss of our favourite animal; the loss of a future we hoped for; the loss of what we thought was true; the loss of the childhood we yearned for; the loss of a friendship; the loss of a job; or the loss of our sense of self. Losses can be big or small; prominent losses that everyone can see or a thousand tiny moments of loss hidden in the shadows.

Loss is also connected to separation, rejection and abandonment. Especially in our younger years, if we experience a significant loss, for example, of a parent, without the full truth and perspective of adult wisdom, we can misinterpret loss. It can cause additional pain and suffering as we create beliefs such as, 'I wasn't wanted', 'Everyone leaves me' or 'I am not enough'. We can also experience grief if we feel as though we don't belong. The unconscious desire to fit in, find meaning and be loved drives us, and when we don't get what we need, it can cause us grief.

Grief of all shapes and sizes, roots and directions is significant. Bring compassion to your thoughts and actions when navigating life with grief in your sidecar.

Trauma

We all experience trauma in different ways. You and I could both be in the same car crash, and we would interpret it differently based on our mindset created in childhood. One of us could walk away thinking, 'The world's not a safe place', and the other thinking, 'Nothing ever goes well'. A belief or decision is either created or reinforced in every experience we have. We might already believe, 'I am not safe', and the traumatic experience only affirms that this is the correct belief to have.

How we react to a traumatic experience also differs based on our nervous system. If we are in a grounded, stable and calm place, our stress level will be elevated, but it shouldn't take too long for us to come back to neutral. On the other hand, if we were already stressed and overwhelmed with negative emotions, an additional traumatic experience might push our mind, body and soul over the edge.

In our early years, we are not equipped with awareness or the tools to support resilience, so we often repress experiences and forget they happened. These difficult experiences are used to create safety strategies and shape our mindset. This then influences every experience thereafter as it is the filter we view life through.

As we explored in Chapter 5, staying grounded and stable supports our resilience. We are able to withstand levels of challenges that peak and trough without too much impact or damage.

PTSD

PTSD, or post-traumatic stress disorder, is when we become overwhelmed by a traumatic experience, causing our stress response to stay activated long after the threat has passed. PTSD can occur shortly after the trauma, or it can be delayed and appear long after the event. If left unsupported it can get worse over time, so it is important to identify it as early as possible and seek help.

There are many symptoms of PTSD to watch out for, including:

- Intense and painful memories, flashbacks or nightmares.
- Difficulty falling asleep or being awake for hours in the middle of the night.
- Physical sensations such as elevated heart rate, difficulty breathing, panic and anxiety, nausea, dizziness and chest pain.
- Emotional symptoms such as disconnection and numbing of emotions, anxiety, panic attacks, feeling unsafe, being easily startled, socially withdrawing, a desire to hide and guilt and shame.
- Mental symptoms such as a loud, critical voice, negative thoughts on loop, loss of interest in things once enjoyed, self-blame and difficulty with focus and concentration.

Triggers

Traumatic experiences are held in sort of trauma time-capsules. Imagine a medical gelatine capsule, where each end encases a trauma and holds it inside. Inside is the memory of the event, the emotions created and the belief or decision made in that moment.

Sometimes the capsule opens itself and the memory inside floods the conscious mind, creating the flashback. When it does this, the brain is trying to seek resolution for the experience. The body knows there is still some energy being held or attached to the memory and wants to release it.

An external stimulus can also trigger the opening of the capsule. We may have pushed the capsule to the side or buried it deep and one day something someone says, or the smell of a particular perfume, or a movie plot line or an advert on TV will call forth the capsule, open it and flood your body with all those sensations you've worked so hard to forget.

When either of these events happens, we can feel the experience as if it is happening to us all over again. Our mind doesn't know the difference between reality and the memories, so as we relive these memories, our energy system is reliving them as if they are happening in real time. This is when safety becomes very important.

Thinking of triggers as a hook or attachment to the past can be helpful. Being triggered is a reminder that there is an unhealed wound seeking acknowledgement, acceptance, forgiveness and love. It might help to think of triggers as opportunities. The more healing work we do on specific memories, emotions and beliefs, the less we are triggered, as the attachment to the past will not exist. Gradually, the mind will find the resolution it was seeking.

Tapping for Grief and PTSD

Tapping is proven to be a powerful way to ease PTSD symptoms. The most significant trial was conducted in 2023 by clinical and health psychologist Peta Stapleton, science writer Dawson Church and their colleagues[1]. Their study of war veterans found that after six treatments and a six-month follow-up period, 90 per cent of the participants no longer qualified for a clinical diagnosis of PTSD.

Tapping by yourself in a self-help capacity can reduce PTSD symptoms. However, I also suggest working with a qualified EFT practitioner on the deeper and root cause of the PTSD and the original trauma or multiple negative experiences.

Before doing this exercise, take a few minutes to connect with the energy of grief and any PTSD symptoms in your body. Think of a particular loss or trauma while you are tapping, but remember that you are completely safe. Notice any pains or tension you feel.

Tune in, find the emotion, give it a colour and location, and rate the intensity from 0–10. Take three deep breaths, and follow the set-up and sequence, inserting your own wording as you wish:

SET-UP STATEMENT (TAPPING ON THE SIDE OF THE HAND):

Even though I feel black grief in my lungs because I am in so much pain and feel a deep sense of loss, I choose to forgive, love and accept myself anyway.

Even though I have this black grief in my lungs that I've been carrying for a while, and I don't know how to let it go, I choose to forgive, love and accept myself anyway.

Even though I feel the heavy impact of trauma on my body, and I feel so low and anxious at times, I choose to forgive, love and accept myself anyway.

Grief and PTSD Tapping Sequence

Commence tapping, starting at the top of the head and going down the points:

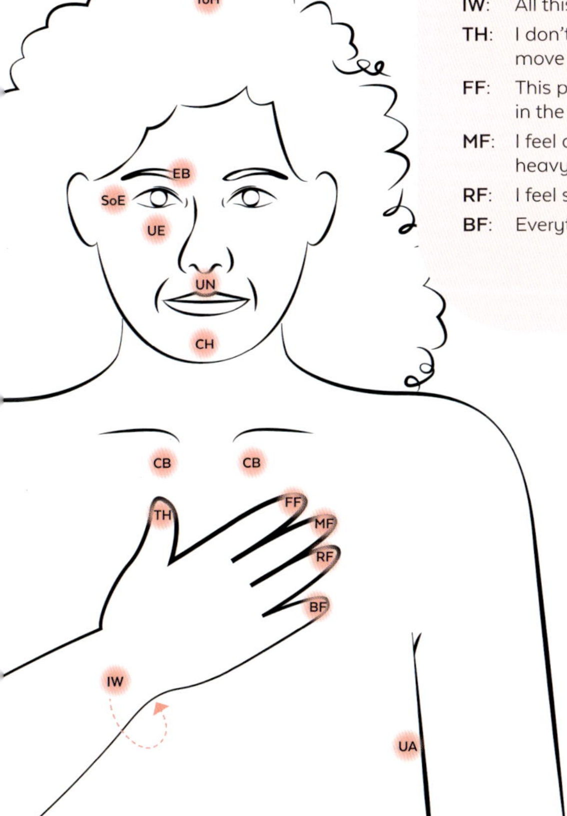

ToH: This black grief in my lungs

EB: All this black grief

SoE: It feels so heavy

UE: So hard to shift

UN: I feel such loss

CH: This pain is so present

CB: I feel there is nowhere for it to go

UA: A void of deep grief within me

IW: All this pain and sadness

TH: I don't know how to let go and move forward

FF: This pain is keeping me stuck in the past

MF: I feel anxious with this heavy energy

RF: I feel so on edge

BF: Everything feels so uncertain

ToH: I have felt out of control

EB: I have spiralled downward

SoE: Things feel so depressing at times

UE: It's hard for me to see the way out

UN: It's hard for me to feel joy

CH: Maybe my heart has closed to joy and love

CB: But what if I could keep my heart open?

UA: What if I could take myself out of this frozen space?

IW: What if I can learn to live with this loss?

TH: What if I can let some of this pain go?

FF: What if I can move on from this trauma?

MF: Maybe I can start letting go now

RF: Maybe I can give myself permission to let go

BF: I don't want to hold onto this pain any more

ToH: I choose now to start letting go of this grief

EB: I let go of these heavy energies on my chest

SoE: I let go of the black grief in my lungs

UE: I allow myself to unfreeze

UN: It is safe now

CH: I am not going through this trauma again

CB: Time has moved on

UA: I have moved forward

IW: It is time for all of my soul to catch up

TH: I release myself from where I froze

FF: I allow myself to accept this situation

MF: I don't like it but I can start accepting it happened

RF: And I cannot change what happened

BF: So, I am ready to move forward and let go even more

ToH: Letting go of this shock and frozen energy
EB: Letting go of the anxiety and fear
SoE: Letting go of the need to control the outcome
UE: I surrender to the letting-go process
UN: I know it is time to start and continue letting go
CH: There is a lot for me to let go of
CB: And I can handle it all
UA: I am strong enough to let go and move forward
IW: I release as much as I can in this moment
TH: There is more work to do and that is okay
FF: I give myself the compassion and time I need
MF: I forgive myself for feeling this way
RF: I love all parts of me, even the parts in pain
BF: I am love and I am whole, just as I am

CHECK-IN

How are you feeling now? Rate yourself on a scale of 0–10. What number are you? Has the intensity dropped? Does your body feel any lighter? Did any memories surface? Feel free to repeat the exercise.

CHAPTER 8

Tapping for Forgiveness

Hatred never ceases by hatred, but by love alone is healed. This is the ancient and eternal law. – *The Buddha*

Forgiveness

The American Psychological Association defines forgiveness as: a voluntary transformation of your feelings, attitudes and behaviour, so that you are no longer dominated by resentment and can express compassion, generosity or the like toward the person who wronged you.

FORGIVENESS IS A KEY PART OF LETTING GO AND IT IS CRUCIAL TO OUR HEALING JOURNEY.

Forgiveness is a key part of letting go and it is crucial to our healing journey. Often, we hold onto our anger, frustration, rage, bitterness, guilt, shame and sadness about a situation for many reasons, which may include expecting it to hurt the other person. In that case, all we are doing is holding tightly to this energy and ultimately it is hurting only us.

We can also be resistant to the idea of forgiving ourselves. Societal conditioning puts a huge amount of pressure on us, meaning we hold ourselves to very high standards. This can result in internalized punishment through our critical voice and the storing of negative emotions.

Buddhist philosophy also references forgiveness as a healing pathway, understanding that both forgiveness and love can bring about the peace we seek. Forgiveness is considered something that can help someone release the suffering of the past. It helps us find compassion, courage and integrity to release ourselves of the suffering of the past. It helps us let go of the chains and shackles we have around our heart.

Often the shift in perspective helps us to see the bigger picture and sometimes we can see what was going on for the other person at that time. Just a little bit of awareness can lead to the desire to forgive. It is a very conscious decision that you can take when you are ready.

Bringing forgiveness into your life not only affects your emotions but it can also have a mental and physiological impact. A 2014 study[1] by psychology professor Nathaniel Wade and his colleagues focused on reviewing the efficacy of psychotherapeutic forgiveness interventions to help people forgive others, found that these interventions are associated with significant reductions in depression and anxiety.

FORGIVENESS IS A VERY CONSCIOUS DECISION THAT YOU CAN MAKE WHEN YOU ARE READY.

Condoning Versus Forgiving

It is important to acknowledge and understand the difference between condoning and forgiving. Some won't entertain the idea of forgiving because they mix up the action with condoning the behaviour.

Understandably, many people who have been abused and victimized really struggle with forgiveness. It is not an easy thing to forgive your abuser or people who have hurt you.

Condoning is saying that this bad behaviour was or is okay, and often allows the situation to continue, whereas forgiveness is not saying that the behaviour was acceptable. Instead forgiveness is a process of releasing the internal negative energies generated from that experience. It is much more about the forgiver than the person being forgiven.

Allow yourself to get to a place of forgiveness in your own space and time and seek support if this feels very far away from you. You might like to do some further research into the concept of forgiveness or need someone else to guide your perspective to help you forgive and let go.

Tapping for Forgiveness

Tapping aids forgiveness by generating awareness, connecting with the emotion, shifting perspective, observing empathy or providing compassion, and then letting go. Tapping hacks your brain, encouraging safety that enables energy to be released. There is such relief to be had if and when you go there.

This tapping sequence is for releasing anger from an event or person you can't forgive, or you can use it to forgive yourself.

Before doing this exercise, take a few minutes to connect with the energy resulting from lack of forgiveness. What is the emotion that rises when you're struggling to forgive? Are you feeling anger toward them? Is it sadness? Is it rage, frustration or disappointment? Notice any pains or tension in particular areas.

Tune in, find the emotion, give it a colour and location, and rate the intensity from 0–10. Take three deep breaths, and follow the set-up and sequence, inserting your own wording where this feels right:

SET-UP STATEMENT (TAPPING ON THE SIDE OF THE HAND):

Even though I'm holding all this red rage in my body, when I think about this event/person I can't accept or forgive, I choose to forgive, love, and accept myself anyway.

Even though I've got this red rage in my chest, when I think of this person or time in my life, or even myself because I struggle to accept and forgive this issue, I choose to forgive, love, and accept myself anyway.

Even though I've got this red rage in my chest, I'm struggling to let this event or person go. I've held this for quite some time. I know it's not serving me. And I choose to forgive, love and accept myself anyway.

Forgiveness Tapping Sequence

Commence tapping, starting at the top of the head and going down the points:

ToH: This red rage in my chest

EB: All this red rage in my chest

SoE: So much rage

UE: I've been holding this rage for a long time

UN: When I think about this event/ person

CH: I just feel anger that I am holding on to

CB: I've struggled to accept that this happened to me

UA: I've struggled to accept this whole experience

IW: And I know that this acceptance and forgiveness would be good for me

TH: But part of me doesn't want to let go

FF: Part of me doesn't want to accept

MF: Part of me doesn't want to forgive

RF: What if forgiving means I'm condoning what happened to me?

BF: I don't want to do that

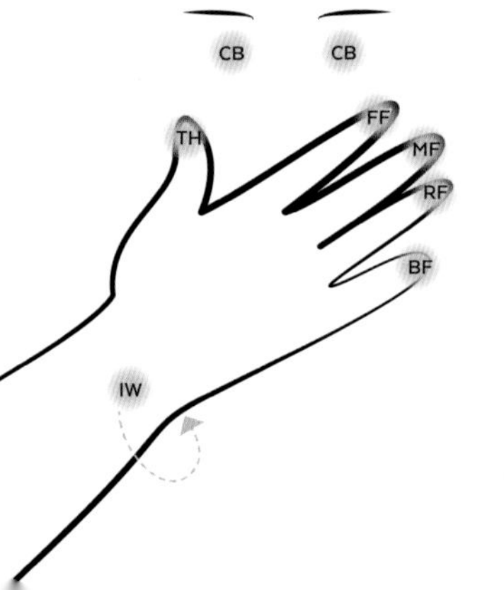

ToH: I'm not condoning that thing that happened
EB: But I accept all parts of me
SoE: I accept the parts that want to forgive and move on
UE: And the parts that want to hold on to this anger
UN: Even though part of me wants to forgive
CH: And another part of me wants to feel this pain
CB: I accept all these parts of me now
UA: Even though I'm resisting to forgive fully
IW: Resisting to accept fully that this thing happened
TH: I accept how I feel
FF: I know the part of me that won't let go or is struggling to let go
MF: It is just the wounded part of me
RF: This experience hurt me so much
BF: And it's okay to not want to let go

ToH: But maybe I could look at this in a different way
EB: I'm holding on to all this pain
SoE: It was painful, I suffered and I am still suffering
UE: It's weighing me down
UN: Leaving me feeling powerless
CH: Holding on to this is hurting me
CB: What if I could be free of these emotions?
UA: What if I could accept what happened?
IW: What if I could let go of the pain and the trauma?
TH: What if I could be free of the shock and the rage?
FF: Maybe now is the time to let it all go
MF: I'm opening myself up to forgiveness now
RF: Choosing now to release all this rage from my body
BF: I choose to accept what has happened in the past

ToH: I forgive this event, that person or people

EB: And I am open to forgiving myself

SoE: For any wrongs that I have done in the past too

UE: For any time that I have hurt someone else without realizing

UN: Or hurt someone else on purpose

CH: That's just come from my wounded self

CB: And I'm sorry for doing that

UA: So I choose to forgive all people

IW: I forgive all the people that have wronged me

TH: I forgive all situations and experiences

FF: And I forgive myself, because I was doing the best that I could at that time

MF: I created a safety strategy for myself

RF: To try to protect myself from future pain

BF: So, I forgive all involved. I forgive myself

CHECK-IN

How are you feeling now? Rate yourself on a scale of 0–10. What number are you? Has the intensity dropped? Does your body feel any lighter? Did any memories surface? Feel free to repeat the exercise.

CHAPTER 9

Tapping for Guilt, Shame and Blame

Guilt and shame are tethers to the past, misguiding us toward self-blame.

Guilt, Shame and Blame

These are some of the densest, heaviest and most destructive energies we can hold.

We explored the definition of shame and guilt briefly on page 24, but shame is internalized and personal, as in, 'I am bad'. As Brené Brown outlines in her book *Atlas of the Heart,* shame is a more personal emotion because it acts as a reflection of the self.[1] When we feel shame, we believe we are not good enough. In contrast, guilt is more external because it is tied to our behaviour. For example, 'I did a bad thing', versus 'I am bad'.

Guilt and shame are tethers to the past, misguiding us toward self-blame. It is hard to move forward when we are constantly blaming ourselves for things we've said or done in the past. These feelings limit us by preventing us from being present and enjoying life to the fullest. It is also impossible to love ourselves unconditionally when we are feeling self-hatred or self-judgement. We'll discuss unconditional love more in Chapter 16.

At the root of these feelings will be experiences that created beliefs in your subconscious. These emotions serve as reminders of unhealed traumas that are still heavily influencing your day-to-day life. One other important fact to bear in mind about shame is that it relies on secrecy. Having someone see our faults, provide empathy and not reject us is a very healing experience. It can remind us that we are loved and accepted for who we are: our true authentic selves.

HAVING SOMEONE SEE OUR FAULTS, PROVIDE EMPATHY AND NOT REJECT US IS A VERY HEALING EXPERIENCE.

Reframing Guilt, Shame and Blame

YOU ARE NOT TO BLAME FOR WHAT HAS HAPPENED TO YOU IN YOUR LIFE.

'It wasn't my fault'. This is a very powerful reframe to use when you are looking back at past events in your life. As children we often internalize everything that happens in our lives as our fault. We cannot see the bigger picture and we feel our actions have a direct consequence on what happens in our lives, even though there are many different aspects influencing those situations.

I want you to take a moment now to let this sink in: you are not to blame for what has happened to you in your life. Very few of us set out consciously to hurt ourselves or others. Therefore, most hurt inflicted is a result of subconscious strategies for ensuring safety, love and a sense of belonging. We have not consciously chosen them. If you can see that your safety strategies are a biproduct of circumstance and external factors that you have no control over, it is a lot easier to release the blame you place on yourself and thus the guilt and shame that you carry. Letting go of the blame allows us to take accountability for our actions going forward. These two can also coexist; we cannot be to blame, but we can take ownership and responsibility.

Tapping For Guilt, Shame and Blame

Before doing this exercise, I invite you to think about an experience or a person that has caused you to feel these negative emotions. What emotions are you feeling? Do you notice any pains or tension in particular areas.

Tune in, find the emotion, give it a colour and location, and rate the intensity from 0–10. Then, take three deep breaths, and follow the set-up steps and tapping sequence, inserting your own wording where this feels right:

SET-UP STATEMENT (TAPPING ON THE SIDE OF THE HAND):

Even though I feel the black energy of guilt, shame and blame in my chest, I choose to forgive, love and accept myself anyway.

Even though I'm holding this guilt, shame and blame in my chest, I know some of this is not mine, I choose to forgive, love and accept myself anyway.

Even though I'm holding this black guilt, shame and blame in my chest, I choose to forgive, love and accept myself anyway.

Guilt, Shame and Blame Tapping Sequence

Commence tapping, starting at the top of the head and going down the points:

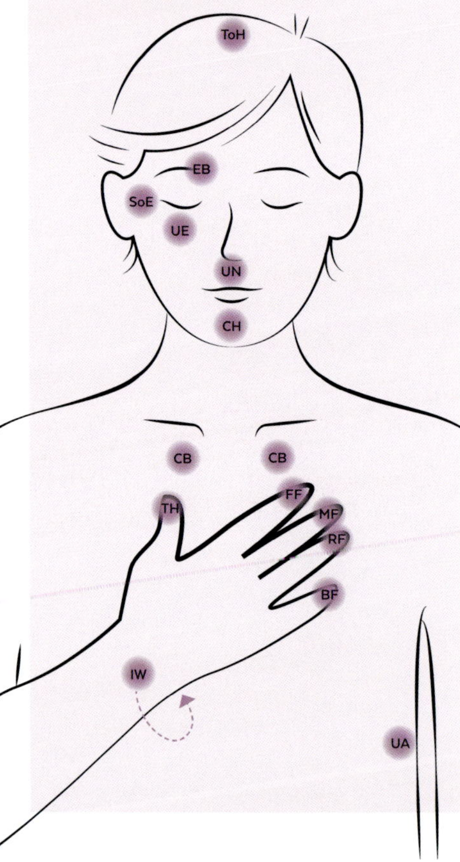

ToH: This guilt in my chest
EB: So much guilt in my body
SoE: I've done things I'm not proud of
UE: I've said things I'm not proud of
UN: So much guilt I've caused myself
CH: And guilt that I've absorbed and inherited
CB: This guilt that isn't mine
UA: And all this guilt that is mine
IW: Weighing heavy on my body
TH: Maybe I was just a young child
FF: Or maybe I didn't know any better
MF: Maybe I was acting from my wounded self
RF: Maybe I was just trying to keep myself safe
BF: Maybe I didn't have the support that I needed

ToH: Maybe I was doing the best that I could
EB: With the knowledge and understanding I had at that time
SoE: Maybe it's okay to let myself off the hook
UE: Maybe it's time to let it all go
UN: I choose to release and let go of all the guilt in my body
CH: Letting go of this guilt
CB: It doesn't serve me
UA: There is no purpose to my guilt
IW: And as I heal and change
TH: I know I won't make those same mistakes again
FF: I made mistakes I'm not proud of
MF: But I can't change the past
RF: All I can do is forgive myself and let g
BF: I release all remaining guilt now

ToH: Tuning in now to the energy of shame and blame
EB: There's no need to hold this shame or blame
SoE: I've learned the lesson from my experiences
UE: Maybe I've learned I don't want to repeat certain behaviours
UN: Maybe this shame and blame didn't start with me
CH: Maybe it's not mine to carry
CB: Blaming others isn't helping me
UA: Blaming myself isn't helping me
IW: I don't need to blame myself any more
TH: The lessons I've learned through my experiences
FF: Have shaped me into who I am today
MF: It's okay now to let it all go, too
RF: Choosing now to let go of all the shame and blame
BF: Letting it all go

ToH: Letting go of blame and shame from every cell in my body
EB: It's no one's fault
SoE: It's not my fault
UE: It's just what happened
UN: I am perfectly imperfect
CH: I am imperfectly perfect
CB: I am always doing the best I can
UA: I am not flawed or unworthy
IW: I don't need fixing
TH: I am evolving
FF: It's safe to let love in
MF: It's safe to feel love
RF: It's safe to belong
BF: It's safe to be here now in this moment, in this love

CHECK-IN

How are you feeling now? Rate yourself on a scale of 0–10. What number are you? Has the intensity dropped? Does your body feel any lighter? Did any memories surface? Feel free to repeat the exercise.

Zero-guilt Policy: A Four-step Zero-guilt Formula

I try to operate a zero-guilt policy to prevent myself holding on to guilt for too long. While feelings of guilt can be useful to give us a warning sign that something isn't right, which can determine where we can make changes in our lives and help us identify what needs to be healed, it is important not to hold onto those feelings for too long. In moments of intense guilt, we are not living in our flow state, full of self-love and compassion; we are living in a state of fear, self-hatred, judgement, sadness and despair.

1

Question where the feeling has come from

Firstly, acknowledge what has happened or what you feel you've done. Then question the feeling. Is this something you have genuinely done wrong, or is this some conditioning making you feel that you should feel guilty?

2

If it is a genuine error, own it

Get curious as to why you reacted the way you did, how it might have affected the other person and how you could have acted instead. Apologize and repair if appropriate. Investigate what belief you're holding that made you act from fear, not love. What pain are you still holding that contributed to this reaction that signals you need more comfort and love?

If this guilt is not yours and is a result of collective conditioning, recognize the external force that is influencing your emotions and forgive yourself for that. Most likely you were not aware, and you've been conditioned to please others above all else and your reaction was a learned, unconscious behaviour.

3

Forgive yourself and let go

Use tapping or other tools to feel, acknowledge, forgive and release the energy that was causing you the discomfort. Tune in to the emotion, locate it in your body, understand why it's there and invite your body to let it go. Use the tapping sequences in this chapter to help you.

4

Make a plan to grow

Look for the lesson from the experience. What could you take with you into the future? How would you like to behave in this kind of situation instead? Take the opportunity to learn from it and try to put these learnings into practice next time.

STEP 3:
THE DEEPER JOURNEY

What remains hidden has power, so this step helps us heal and embrace the forgotten parts of ourselves through compassion and courage. Using tapping and visualization, we begin by working with our inner child. Next, should this apply to us, we reflect on the experience of womanhood and motherhood, celebrating and healing the complex stories that can shape our identities, and holding space for the trials that may challenge us. Finally, we confront our shadow self, deepening our self-awareness, compassion and resilience to make space for lasting, transformative change.

CHAPTER 10

Tapping into Your Inner Child

Your younger self is often stuck in a difficult period in time, awaiting resolution, acknowledgement, love and release.

Your Inner Child

You may have heard of the term inner child before. Although the term was originally coined by Swiss psychiatrist Carl Jung over 100 years ago, it has become very popular in recent years. You may have even done some work in this area already. But even if you have, I'd like you to consider how you can use tapping to support those earlier versions of you.

From my experience as an EFT practitioner, the inner child surfaces in sessions because of a wounding of some kind, whether that is caused by separation, abandonment, neglect, abuse, feeling unloved or as a result of a trauma. As we have learned already in this book, these experiences can create lasting impact on our psyche by limiting our beliefs, and also in our energy field through the creation of negative emotions.

Although the term 'inner child' was created to recognise the importance of experiences in childhood, I like to think of my inner child as every past version of me, so this chapter is designed to speak to a previous version of you from any age that requires support. Your inner child work may speak to a conscious memory, or general feelings you associate with yourself from that age. For instance, there are versions of my inner child that are happy and content, and there are also versions that are wounded or frozen in trauma.

YOUR INNER CHILD WORK MAY SPEAK TO A CONSCIOUS MEMORY, OR GENERAL FEELINGS YOU ASSOCIATE WITH YOURSELF FROM THAT AGE.

Inner Child Impact

How do you know if you are suffering in adulthood because of unresolved past trauma? The answer can be easy or complex. Obvious, visible traumas, such as the loss of a parent, are quite easy to identify. Less visible but potentially extremely damaging traumas, such as not receiving the unconditional love, affection and attention you needed as a child, are much harder to identify.

Consider the following questions:

Question		Explanation
1. Do you often experience strong emotional reactions to difficult situations in adulthood?	→	Often our unloved or angry inner child might respond disproportionately to present-day challenges.
2. Do you struggle to accept current situations, and therefore can't let go and move on?	→	Sometimes, we can't let go of a current situation because it is linked to a much earlier event we are still suffering from or impacted by.
3. Do you feel stuck with fear when thinking of the future, or when it comes to making choices?	→	We can feel paralyzed because of residual shock and fear held by our inner child.
4. Is it hard for you to create and stick to boundaries when you want to be liked and loved by everyone?	→	Our inner child had to adapt to all situations, and sometimes that meant we abandoned our own needs and true self.
5. Do you find it hard to be vulnerable and admit when you need support, and then struggle to accept it when it comes?	→	It can feel unsafe to be vulnerable and often our inner child had to become very independent to survive.
6. Do you have a history of unhealthy relationships in adulthood?	→	Our unhealed inner child is looking for love externally, which can lead to co-dependency and unhealthy relationship behaviours or decisions.

7. Have you suppressed and repressed feelings in childhood and beyond because it did not feel safe to share them?		Often our inner child is still holding unexpressed feelings.
8. Do you have a loud critical voice that reminds you of your mother or father?		Sometimes our critical voice takes on the persona of our mother or father to protect our inner child from further pain or suffering.

It is likely you've identified with one or several of these, and please be reassured that the majority of people could do with supporting their inner child to some degree. This awareness and supportive work will be useful on so many levels.

Working with Your Inner Child

There are many ways to connect with your inner child, from journalling to meditation, and visualization to talking therapy. I find tapping so effective when supporting the inner child as it brings somatic release and safety programming to the nervous system (see page 30) while powerfully acknowledging the suffering we are still holding on to from a particular age or memory.

As we've already established, safety is extremely important in the healing process. It allows the body to let go physically of negative energy and limiting beliefs. Working with our inner child is the same, but safety can be even more crucial because in a lot of situations, our inner child didn't feel safe, either physically or in relation to their sense of self.

Inner Child Visualization Exercise

1. *Start by getting comfortable, and then focus on your breath. Bring all of your awareness into your body and try to elongate your breath a little, guiding your body back to calm. Set an intention that you wish to connect with the younger self within you that needs the most support right now.*

2. *Imagine yourself transported to a safe space in nature, somewhere you've been before or somewhere that is a fiction of your imagination. Take a few moments to look or sense around you, and breathe it all in. When you are ready, invite your inner child to meet you here in this safe space.*

3. *Welcome them when they appear, and explain that you've come to witness their pain, and acknowledge all they have been through. Greet them with kindness and compassion. Take in their appearance, sense their emotions, give them a little time. Ask them what they are feeling right now, or what's going on for them at this time in their life. Be open and receptive to witnessing and acknowledging their experience.*

4. *If it feels comfortable, you can reach out and touch them, sharing affection so they know they are not alone. You could draw them in close to a hug, hold them on your lap or sit opposite them and hold hands. Ask your inner child questions about their current situation and ask them what beliefs or decisions they made about themself off the back of the experiences they are having at this age.*

5. *This is a good opportunity to coach them a little with the wisdom and hindsight you can offer them now as an adult. What did they need to know about this*

situation that they could not have possibly known at the time? Do they have shame or guilt that needs to be released? What could you say to them that would allow them to let go of the negative energy or belief they are still holding?

6. *Get imaginative in your support. Picture things that will help them let go, such as inviting a colour to surround them or asking them to throw their feelings and beliefs into a fire. Alternatively, invite them to partake in the upcoming tapping sequence in this chapter with you.*

7. *You could also visualize showing them pictures of your life now, so they know they can trust you and see that things work out in their future. Even if it is not all a bed of roses, they might need to know that you survived certain experiences. Ask them what they need and then allow that to play out in your visualization. Parents might need to enter the picture, conversations might need to be had with them, and you might need to hand back some responsibilities. Let your younger self guide the way.*

8. *When you feel they have released the negative energy or belief, tell them you are here for them and will come back and check in on how they are doing. If they are struggling to let go, come back another time and ask them to share what they are holding on to. You might need to alleviate some fear for them. Before you leave, wrap them up in a bubble of light or colour, or leave them with an angel or safe family member so they feel loved and know they are not alone.*

9. *Return to this exercise regularly to check in on different ages or versions of your inner child.*

Tapping for Your Inner Child

Tapping is a great way to bring acknowledgement, compassion and support to your inner child. Feel free to do the visualization exercise in this chapter before the tapping sequence, or you can go straight in with the sequence if you feel comfortable to do so.

Either way, think of a previous version of you – at any age – that you feel needs support with this technique. Alternatively, if a memory surfaces, you can tune in to that. You may find multiple inner childs come to you at different ages, so be open and just allow whatever surfaces to be.

This sequence is a little different from the others in this book because we are going to talk to our inner child while tapping. We can also rate it a bit differently, too. Look at your inner child, or the version of you in this memory, and rate their happiness or contentment as a percentage. The goal with this exercise is to increase their joy or contentment percentage.

SET-UP STATEMENT (TAPPING ON THE SIDE OF THE HAND):

Even though you are struggling to feel safe, happy and content, I see you, I hear you and I am here to take care of you.

Even though you are going through a lot, and you feel scared and lonely, I see you, I hear you and I am here to take care of you.

Even though you feel lost, stuck, invisible and unloved, I see you, I hear you and I am here to take care of you.

Inner Child Tapping Sequence

Commence tapping, starting at the top of the head and going down the points:

ToH: All this fear and suffering

EB: You feel so alone

SoE: You can't share how you feel

UE: You've hidden away your feelings

UN: It wasn't safe to speak your truth

CH: You've been through so much

CB: You don't understand why you have these feelings

UA: You don't understand why things feel so hard

IW: You fear you'll be stuck here forever

TH: Maybe you feel this is your fault

FF: Maybe you think you've done something wrong

MF: Maybe you don't feel good enough

RF: Maybe you are afraid you'll be abandoned

BF: Maybe you are afraid of being judged

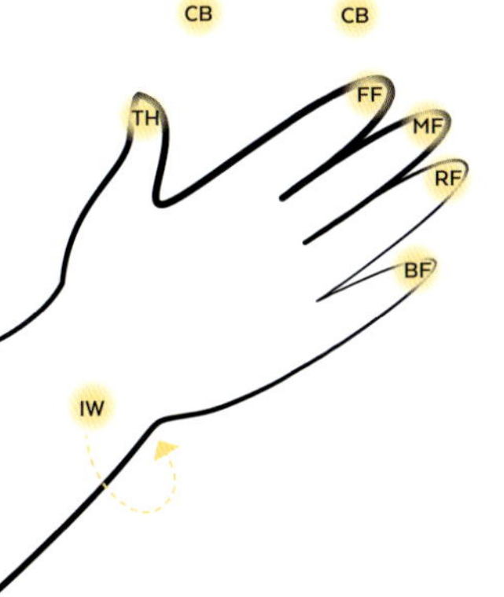

ToH: All you've ever wanted is to be loved
EB: To belong, and be seen and understood
SoE: To be held and supported
UE: It's not your fault you feel so sad and alone
UN: You've hidden yourself away to stay safe
CH: You've been trying so hard to make others happy
CB: You've lost connection with who you really are
UA: You've been trying to be the good child
IW: I'm here now to help you feel seen and heard
TH: Because it was not your fault
FF: You did nothing wrong
MF: And you need to know how loved you are
RF: There is nothing wrong with you
BF: You are perfect just as you are

ToH: It's time now to let go of these emotions
EB: Because you deserve to feel good
SoE: Choosing together now to let go of all this pain
UE: Letting go now of all of the suffering
UN: Releasing all the fear you've been carrying
CH: There is nothing to be afraid of
CB: Because you can cope beautifully
UA: With whatever comes your way
IW: Releasing all the loneliness you've been carrying
TH: You might think you are alone, but you aren't
FF: So many people love you
MF: You have so many friends
RF: You are so supported
BF: And I support you

ToH: Let's choose now to feel good
EB: We can feel good about ourselves
SoE: We work together as a team
UE: We can get through anything
UN: We can see the joy in our lives
CH: We feel grateful for it all
CB: We can relax and surrender
UA: We can feel safe and secure
IW: We can feel confident
TH: Because we do the best we can
FF: And we are enough
MF: Exactly as we are
RF: In every moment
BF: We are pure love

CHECK-IN

How are you feeling now? Rate yourself on a scale of 0–10. What number are you? Has the intensity dropped? Does your body feel any lighter? Did any memories surface? Feel free to repeat the exercise.

CHAPTER 11

Tapping into Womanhood

The path to womanhood is both a powerful and complex journey, where often expectations of society clash with our evolving sense of self.

A Rite of Passage

Evolving from a girl into a woman can be a very complicated, confusing and lonely time. I acknowledge that the concept of girlhood and womanhood is vast and inclusive, multiple and wonderful; everyone has a different experience, especially people who have been socialized as women and girls but possess different gender identities, or vice versa. One thing that we can all acknowledge is the many challenges and pressures that all women and girls face.

The path to womanhood is both a powerful and complex journey, where often expectations of society clash with our evolving sense of self. This rite of passage is marked by both beautiful and painful moments. Very often girls have to navigate the milestones associated with society's idea of womanhood all on their own. For some people, these milestones might include puberty, sexual experiences, first loves and complex friendships.

During our teenage years, we experience an intense physical evolution. Our body shape changes, menstruation begins, our hormones can make us sensitive and acne may appear. We can start to feel as if we've lost control. This might be the first time we feel shame and confusion about our body, and it can be deeply scarring, especially if we create a limiting belief as a result.

Alongside these physical changes, our place in society also shifts. We can become so much more aware of how we look, comparing ourselves to beautiful people we see online, wanting to be like others, focusing externally on cosmetic beauty. We can start to leave behind the innocent childlike wonder and sense of fun we may have had and now have to navigate a world that tells us how to be. Society, media, family and friends have explicit or covert expectations of us as we move towards womanhood that can lead to feelings of inadequacy, and deeply disconnect us from our awareness of our true selves.

Teenage Traumas

Growing up in Catholic Ireland I experienced a deep sense of shame around the basic facts of life, hiding tampons in my sleeve at school and not wanting anyone to know I had my period. As a result of this, together with a limited access to educational representation and various falling-outs with friends, I have gaps in my memory of some key events that still haunt me to this day. I feel immense shame and regret about some of my actions, but looking back now I know it was because I deeply craved to belong.

I've worked with many women who hadn't realized the impact their teenage years have had on them. They come to me for confidence or to support them with an adult trauma, and so often we end up finding a root cause or event back in the teenage years. How we are treated in these years has significant and lasting impact. We are very impressionable and often vulnerable. We make bad decisions, follow the crowd and can be the butt of gossip or bullying.

Abuse of many kinds is also possible during this time. Abuse leaves long-lasting damage on the mind, body and soul, so if you have suffered abuse, I really recommend having personalized tapping sessions with a practitioner to support you in letting go of the emotions, beliefs and decisions created as a result. I know the thought of doing this might feel hard, or you may have tried lots of things already, but if there is some emotional charge in your body from reading these words, you might have some energy left to clear. Remember, tapping is a safe way of releasing this energy, and you will be in safe hands.

Emotional Residue

Our experiences shape the energy our bodies create, as well as the beliefs and decisions we use every day to make sense of our world. If we've had a difficult and traumatic transition to womanhood through our teenage years, adulthood is also going to be difficult. Our teenage experiences may reinforce beliefs we had already created, or we may have created brand new safety strategies to try to keep us safe. In adulthood, we will then continue to hold the negative energy created and we might find situations repeat themselves.

SUPPORTING OUR TEENAGE SELF RETROSPECTIVELY WITH TAPPING AND INNER CHILD WORK IS SO EFFECTIVE AT HELPING US LET GO.

Supporting our teenage self retrospectively with tapping and inner child work (see pages 118–21) is so effective at helping us let go of that energetic and emotional residue. This frees us up to be less anxious; to have more confidence; to start trusting ourselves and others; to motivate and push ourselves out of our comfort zone; and to start taking control of the direction of our lives with conscious choice and intention.

Tapping for Womanhood

Tapping helps bring compassion and forgiveness to our teenage selves. We may have unconsciously behaved in certain ways to protect ourselves, and we did the best we could with the knowledge and understanding of the world that we had at the time. Let's use this tapping sequence to release and let go of the emotions generated during these formative, vulnerable and crucial years.

Before doing this exercise, take a few minutes to connect with any emotion that has surfaced while reading this chapter, or as you think of your teenage self. Do you feel embarrassed thinking about how you were at this age? Did you experience anything traumatic that you've suppressed? Did you feel lonely and disconnected from others? Notice any pains or tension in particular areas.

Tune in, find the emotion, give it a colour and location, and rate the intensity from 0–10. Then, take three deep breaths, and follow the set-up and sequence, inserting your own wording where this feels right:

SET-UP STATEMENT (TAPPING ON THE SIDE OF THE HAND):

Even though I am still carrying the weight of heavy emotions from my teenage years, I choose to forgive, love and accept myself anyway.

Even though I am burdened by shame, anxiety, regret and self-doubt because of my teenage years, I choose to forgive, love and accept myself anyway.

Even though I still carry loneliness and fear of not belonging from my teenage years, I choose to forgive, love and accept myself anyway.

Womanhood Tapping Sequence

Commence tapping, starting at the top of the head and going down the points:

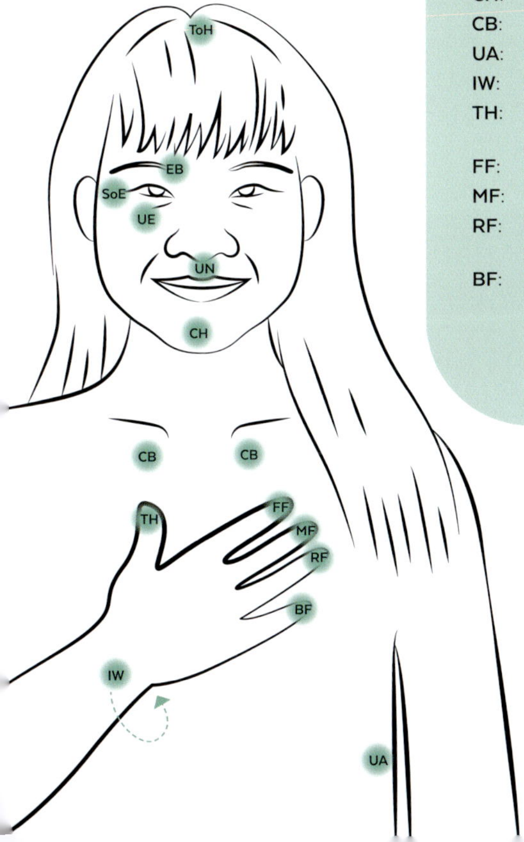

ToH: All these dense, heavy emotions

EB: I've been carrying with me since I was a teenager

SoE: Many experiences have caused me pain

UE: Pain I've tried to hide and forget

UN: Pain I've not been able to fully share

CH: It made me feel so alone

CB: These difficult experiences

UA: Making me feel unworthy

IW: Making me feel not good enough

TH: Making me feel everything is my fault

FF: Making me question myself

MF: Making me forget my true self

RF: These difficult times I've suppressed

BF: And tried to forget

ToH
EB
SoE
UE
UN
CH
CB
CB
TH
FF
MF
RF
BF
IW
UA

ToH: All the shame and regret
EB: For silly things I have done
SoE: For silly things I've said to others
UE: For trying to fit in yet be invisible
UN: For wanting to be seen and heard
CH: I was so afraid of being judged and hurt
CB: Yet I judged myself and others unfairly
UA: I hated myself sometimes
IW: I hated my body
TH: I did some stupid things
FF: I didn't feel good enough
MF: I didn't understand myself
RF: Sometimes I felt like a burden
BF: All this shame, regret and fear

ToH: I felt misunderstood and lonely
EB: I couldn't see that my friends were all in pain too
SoE: We didn't know how to share
UE: We perpetuated all this shame
UN: But it was not our fault
CH: We did not know any other way
CB: Maybe it's time to let all this go
UA: Choosing now to let go of the shame, blame and fear
IW: I forgive myself for all I've done
TH: I was doing the best I could
FF: With the understanding I had at the time
MF: I was just a teenager trying to find my place in the world
RF: I didn't know any other way
BF: I was just trying to get by and survive

ToH: I forgive myself deeply
EB: I let go of all the shame and blame
SoE: I let go of the fear of judgement
UE: I let go of the fear of not belonging
UN: I let go of feeling anxious
CH: I let go of all self-doubt
CB: I choose to back myself
UA: I choose to trust myself
IW: I was enough just as I was
TH: I am enough just as I am now
FF: I send love back to my teenage self
MF: So they know how amazing they are
RF: I forgive and support them
BF: I love them so much

CHECK-IN

How are you feeling now? Rate yourself on a scale of 0–10. What number are you? Has the intensity dropped? Does your body feel any lighter? Did any memories surface? Feel free to repeat the exercise.

CHAPTER 12

Tapping into Motherhood

Much like the birth of a child, motherhood brings forth the birth of the mother herself.

The Journey of Motherhood

MOTHERHOOD CAN ACCELERATE OUR HEALING JOURNEY.

There are so many stages that a person passes through on the journey to motherhood. Each stage comes with its own set of hopes and dreams, alongside disappointments as well as fears. It's a potential juxtaposition of experiences and emotions, often unexpected.

I remember deciding at 31 that I felt ready to become a mother, yet had very little awareness of what would lie ahead. Miscarriages and baby loss were not as talked about as they are today, so I headed into the conception journey in ignorant bliss, and in hindsight, that was a good thing. Increased knowledge of the trials of bringing a baby into the world can often add to stress and anxiety during pregnancy.

By the time we reach motherhood, we usually have a well-established psyche and mindset shaped by our experiences. The more adverse childhood experiences (ACEs) we have had in the past, the harder the transition to motherhood is likely to be.[1] How we cope with the highs and lows of the motherhood journey is linked to our past traumas, healing journey and the tools we use to manage our emotions, critical voice and limiting beliefs. Motherhood can accelerate our healing journey, forcing us to confront new aspects, old limitations and heal traumas from the past.

The Vulnerability of Motherhood

Central to the experience of motherhood is vulnerability, yet it is so often hidden or not spoken about. This vulnerability transforms us physically, emotionally, mentally and spiritually. Much like the birth of a child, motherhood brings forth the rebirth of the mother herself – a transformation that cracks us open, shedding old layers of self as we step into this new identity. This rebirth is profound, often unexpected and it reshapes not only how we see ourselves, but also how we move through the world.

Motherhood exposes us in ways we are often unprepared for, as we lose grip on certainty and control. This raw vulnerability opens us to the depths of insecurity and doubt, leaving us to navigate an entirely new landscape of fears, grief, guilt and shame. But just as birth is a process of intense labour followed by the beauty of new life, so too is a mother's rebirth – a journey of discovering new strength, resilience and capacities we never knew we had.

One of the most common limiting beliefs, 'I am not enough', becomes exaggerated as we attempt to live up to idealized expectations of the perfect mother that are impossible to reach. This belief can stem from a difficult birth, struggles with breastfeeding, postpartum body changes or even the overwhelming responsibility of caring for another human being. When the reality of motherhood sets in, many women experience a resurgence of past traumas, unresolved emotions or unhealed wounds, all of which can resurface when we feel most vulnerable. These can also lead to intrusive and unwanted thoughts.

This vulnerability forces us to find a strength we didn't know we had. As with all experiences, we can find the gifts and silver linings. So although becoming a mother is hard and the transition may not be smooth, it is a privilege with sacred beauty that can fill our hearts with love and joy on a whole other level, even if that might not be instantaneous.

The Emotional Rollercoaster

The myriad of emotions felt during this period depends on our resilience to challenges, which is ultimately determined by early and prior experiences that shape our belief system and create a host of stored emotions in our energy field.

Tapping offers two powerful benefits for resilience. Firstly, research on war veterans with PTSD (see page 90) shows that tapping can create cellular-level changes. Specifically, it helps effectively switch off a biological response linked to stress and trauma. Secondly, tapping enhances resilience by helping manage emotions in real time, providing immediate relief and clarity during stressful moments.

TAPPING ENHANCES RESILIENCE BY HELPING MANAGE EMOTIONS IN REAL TIME.

As soon as I had my first EFT session with my practitioner Kate Marillat, I knew this was the tool mothers across the world were crying out for, which led me to create my practice that focuses on supporting mums. Let's examine some of the emotions that arise in motherhood, and suggest a set-up statement for each one that you can use to develop your own tapping script.

Emotions	Set-up Statements
Grief and sadness Mums can grieve the life they had before children, or their loss of freedom or sense of self. The grief of loss through miscarriage, baby loss or birth trauma is also included here. Let tapping support you to carry your grief by lightening the load as much as you are ready to.	Even though I am carrying black grief within my heart because [insert your own wording here], I choose to forgive, love and accept myself anyway.
Guilt and shame Guilt is very common and almost romanticized in society as an indication of what a good mum we are. Yet it can often be conflicting, as society can make us feel guilty for working, guilty for staying at home, guilty for every decision we make. This guilt feeds the, 'I am not good enough' narrative. Tapping helps you let go of the densest energy you can carry.	Even though I hold guilt and shame in my stomach because of the decisions I've made, I choose to forgive, love and accept myself anyway.
Anger, rage and frustration The relentless giving, the lack of thanks, the lack of support and the mental load can all add up into a boiling pot of rage over time if we don't have a healthy way to express how we feel. This unresolved stress is not good for the mind, body or soul. Use tapping to release the pressure valve.	Even though I feel hot red rage in my throat because I give so much and feel so underappreciated, I choose to forgive, love and accept myself anyway.

Overwhelm and burnout

The job of motherhood comes with a set of additional stresses to those we were accustomed to, like a never-ending to-do list, extra admin, increasing bills, the juggling and so much extra pressure, often self-inflicted. Overwhelm leads to burnout (see pages 76–7), so use tapping to bring calm and ground yourself during stressful and overwhelming moments.

Even though I feel the blue pressure of overwhelm and burnout on my shoulders because I never get a break and I always have so much to do, I choose to forgive, love and accept myself anyway.

USE TAPPING TO BRING CALM AND GROUND YOURSELF IN STRESSFUL AND OVERWHELMING MOMENTS.

Tapping for Motherhood

Tapping can support you in so many ways, and learning to tap can give you an incredible self-help tool to support your motherhood journey. You can apply it to every emotion and situation that you find difficult. You can even teach it to your children.

Vulnerability is a superpower, and it can help us open our hearts wide. In this sequence we use tapping to help us acknowledge, accept and embrace our vulnerability.

Before doing this exercise, take a few minutes to connect in with the energy of vulnerability in your body. Are there any associated emotions? Do any specific memories arise? Notice any pains or tension in particular areas.

Tune in, find the emotion, give it a colour and location, and rate the intensity from 0–10. Then, take three deep breaths, and follow the set-up steps and sequence, inserting your own wording where this feels right:

SET-UP STATEMENT (TAPPING ON THE SIDE OF THE HAND):

Even though I feel so vulnerable since becoming a mum, and I feel the weight of responsibility on me is so heavy and my whole body is heavy with black fear and anxiety, I choose to forgive, love and accept myself.

Even though I'm feeling the black weight of the world on my shoulders since becoming a mum, and I'm struggling with so many emotions I didn't know I had and it's making me feel so vulnerable, I choose to forgive, love and accept myself.

Even though this vulnerability makes me question my coping skills, abilities and choices, and I'm scared that I'm just not good enough for my family, I choose to forgive, love and accept myself.

Motherhood Tapping Sequence

Commence tapping, starting at the top of the head and going down the points:

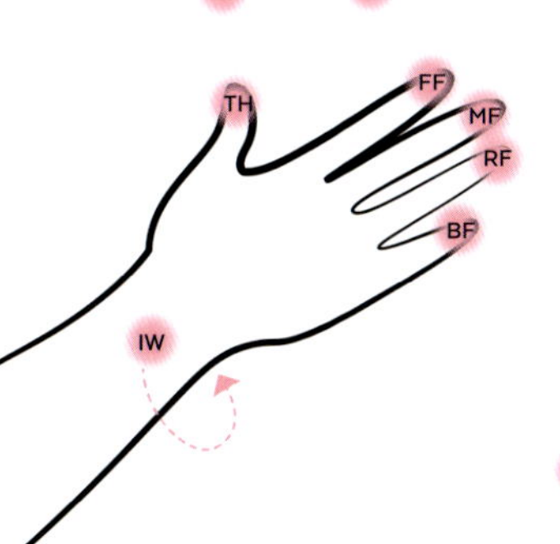

ToH: All this vulnerability in my whole body

EB: This vulnerability is consuming me in blackness

SoE: This black anxiety from feeling vulnerable

UE: I feel it in every cell of my body

UN: I feel a heavy weight on my chest and shoulders

CH: This vulnerability and fear

CB: This need for certainty and control

UA: I'm doubting everything I do

IW: I constantly don't feel good enough

TH: I don't feel like a good mother

FF: Surely good mothers don't feel vulnerable

MF: All these unwanted thoughts in my head

RF: Are making me feel even more vulnerable

BF: I just can't seem to trust myself

ToH: I'm so shaken by becoming a mother

EB: This opening of vulnerability I just didn't expect

SoE: I didn't expect such cultural and societal pressures

UE: I feel like I'm constantly questioning whether I'm doing enough for my family

UN: It feels weak to ask for help

CH: If I ask for help, I'll be considered a bad mother

CB: All these horrible thoughts

UA: All my confidence is gone

IW: I'm so shaken by these dark and heavy feelings

TH: All these intrusive thoughts are upsetting me

FF: I am doubting myself constantly

MF: These feelings make me want to retreat and hide

RF: This blackness in my whole body

BF: I just want to be light

ToH: It's safe for me to start letting go of some of these emotions

EB: I release any negative emotions from my body

SoE: I allow myself to soften and accept help

UE: Accepting I need help makes me strong

UN: This connects me with who I am and what I need

CH: Vulnerability is not a weakness

CB: Being vulnerable takes courage

UA: I am brave

IW: I am enough

TH: I am a good mother

FF: I'm doing the best I can

MF: I have big feelings and that's okay

RF: It's okay to have these feelings

BF: And it's okay to actively let them go

ToH: I don't need to fear these feelings
EB: It's safe to let them move through me
SoE: I allow my vulnerability to be a gift
UE: I let my heart open
UN: I allow myself to feel
CH: I allow myself to let go
CB: Every day is a new day
UA: I can handle whatever comes my way
IW: I choose to feel strong
TH: I choose to feel brave
FF: I believe I am enough
MF: I am a good mother
RF: I am doing the best I can right now
BF: And I love myself for that

CHECK-IN

How are you feeling now? Rate yourself on a scale of 0–10. What number are you? Has the intensity dropped? Does your body feel any lighter? Did any memories surface? Feel free to repeat the exercise.

CHAPTER 13

Tapping into Your Shadow

When we are blind to our shadow, we are blind to the power and potential that lies within us.

The Shadow

This stage of our journey takes us into the shadow. The word 'shadow' in the context we will be exploring in this chapter was brought to our awareness by Carl Jung, and refers to the part of our subconscious where we have stored aspects of ourselves that it was safer to deny and hide away.

Shadow work has become a popular method of healing and integrating the hidden parts of us that we have repressed or denied over time. Shadow as a term can feel intimidating and put some people off going to the deeper recesses of their subconscious, but let me reassure you that this focus of healing is nothing to be scared of, for in the dark you find your light.

It's likely we have interpreted our shadow aspects as unwanted, shameful or negative, hence the desire to suppress and repress them. Society and culture tell us certain thoughts, behaviours and emotions are unacceptable, and it is easy to think of the shadow as inherently bad. However, what we've hidden there is often rooted in trauma, unmet needs, unexpressed emotions and neglected gifts and creativity. For example, if your cheeky and playful self resulted in negative attention at home, and your parents couldn't handle your vivaciousness, then it's likely you started to hide and deny that part of yourself to feel safe, to fit in and to please your parents.

IN THE DARK YOU FIND YOUR LIGHT.

We not only deny aspects of ourselves, but emotions, too. Where does all our unexpressed anger go? It must go somewhere, and we can often find it in the shadow. As the energy we have created alongside aspects of our true personality lingers unknown in the shadow, how can we really know our true selves without uncovering what we've unconsciously sent there? Many of us often feel incomplete, as though we are missing something, and we seek to fill that externally. It might come in the form of love from a partner, or attention from a boss or alcohol on nights out. The truth is that what we are missing is a part of ourselves we've unknowingly denied and forgotten, such as sadness, rage, joy and desires.

This impacts every aspect of our lives because we move further and further away from our true selves the longer we stay unaware. When we are blind to our shadow, we are blind to the power and potential that lies within us.

WHAT WE ARE MISSING IS A PART OF OURSELVES WE'VE UNKNOWINGLY DENIED AND FORGOTTEN.

The Ego

As touched on in Chapter 1, alongside shadow work, it is interesting to bring awareness to our ego. The ego can sneakily sabotage our healing efforts. The ego is our conscious identity, our sense of self and the version of us we present to the world, mask and all. Despite what people might think, our ego is not evil or bad, nor should we be trying to get rid of the ego. Ideally, we are conscious of and work with our ego as ultimately it has been created to help us ride the highs and lows of life.

Ego could be considered as our psychological safety system that has been created to protect us and keep us alive. The ego is not one aspect, but comprised of multiple parts of us collating into one voice. Your ego could comprise the protector, the judge or critic, the hyper achiever, the people pleaser, the victim, the controller and so on. On the surface, this appears positive, but the ego can become overpowered and controlling, especially if your soul's voice has gone quiet or appears withdrawn.

I see the soul and the ego starting with the same purpose and intention, but over time, and in particular following trauma, the ego's voice can become louder, and the soul's voice become quieter. The ego steps in to protect and it gains more power and has a louder, often critical voice that makes it harder to hear our intuitive soul's voice.

Trauma shapes our ego into what it is today, which means we need to bring compassion, forgiveness and love to our ego for it to relinquish some of the safety strategies it put in place, especially those installed as a result of big trauma events.

Remember, the loudest voice is your ego trying to steer you in a different direction; however, the quiet voice or subtle nudge is the quiet wisdom of your intuition.

How the Ego Works

Our ego has various strategies that it uses to protect us, such as:

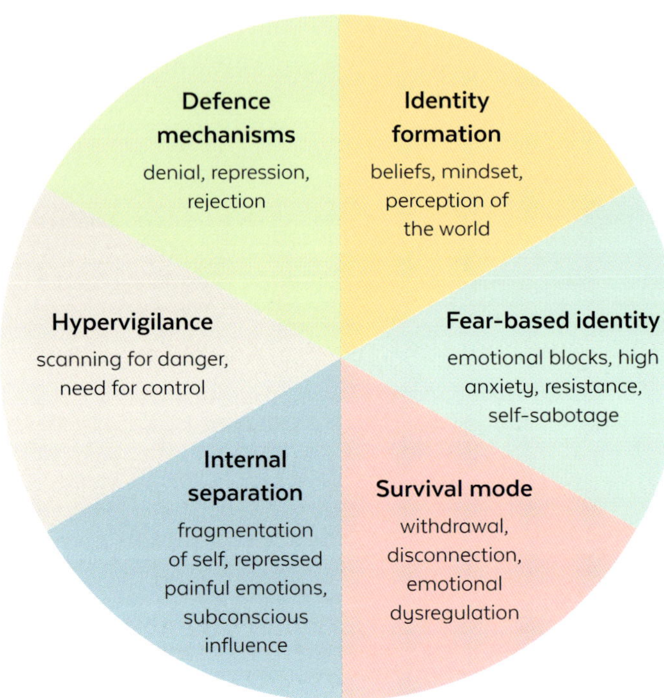

As you can see, these strategies don't lend themselves naturally to openness, willingness to change, compassion, forgiveness and release. The ego is afraid to heal and let go. It avoids pain and suffering as much as possible, so often even getting to a chosen practitioner for support is a feat in itself. Change is not on its agenda; steadfastness to the current status quo is.

Integrating the Shadow

For personal growth, self-acceptance and self-love, facing and reclaiming the parts of ourselves we've disowned will guide us to unity of self and a reunion of our authenticity. By acknowledging the parts of ourselves we've hidden, we reduce their unconscious influence, leading to fewer repetitive negative experiences, greater confidence in ourselves, increased emotional resilience and a sense of inner peace.

You might recognize that every time you tap you are in fact doing shadow work and shadow integration. As we have been learning on this journey, tapping often reveals hidden emotions or beliefs that were created during a traumatic experience, so we are bringing the unconscious to our conscious, or dark to the light, so we can acknowledge, accept, forgive and love.

Let's make this more real with an example about perfectionism and parenting:

A parent who strives for perfection in raising their children may be constantly frustrated when things don't go as planned. This perfectionism might be a shadow aspect, driven by fear of failure or inadequacy, perhaps stemming from their own childhood experiences. Integrating this shadow by acknowledging their need to be perfect and understanding their underlying fears can lead to more self-compassion. As they accept their imperfections, they can model healthier behaviour for their child and foster deeper self-acceptance and emotional resilience. Going one step further and tapping with their inner child (see pages 118–21) on these fears will release the root belief and emotions driving the need for perfectionism in the first place.

Tapping for the Shadow and Ego

Tapping can reveal our shadow parts while circumnavigating the ego. The set-up statement below helps bypass our ego's gatekeeper, allowing us to delve into the subconscious. We can also address the ego directly, encouraging a release of protective mechanisms and allowing for deeper healing. Bringing compassion to our shadow and ego is crucial given these aspects of self and their subconscious behaviour can be rooted in trauma. Reclaiming ostracized parts promotes wholeness and authenticity and frees up energy that was previously suppressing them.

Before doing this exercise, take a few minutes to connect with the parts of yourself that you have unconsciously hidden and suppressed. Can you remember your childlike innocence before you had to adapt and change? What version of you did you have to disown to feel loved? Notice any pains or tension you're experiencing in particular areas.

Tune in, find the emotion, give it a colour and location, and rate the intensity from 0–10. Then, take three deep breaths, and follow the set-up steps and sequence, inserting your own wording where this feels right:

SET-UP STATEMENT (TAPPING ON THE SIDE OF THE HAND):

Even though I have parts of me that are feeling scared, angry and lonely, I choose to support them with compassion and love.

Even though I have parts of me that I've rejected, denied and repressed, I choose to expand my awareness and bring myself back into wholeness.

Even though my ego has worked so hard to keep me safe, I am ready to release what no longer serves me.

Shadow and Ego Tapping Sequence

Commence tapping, starting at the top of the head and going down the points:

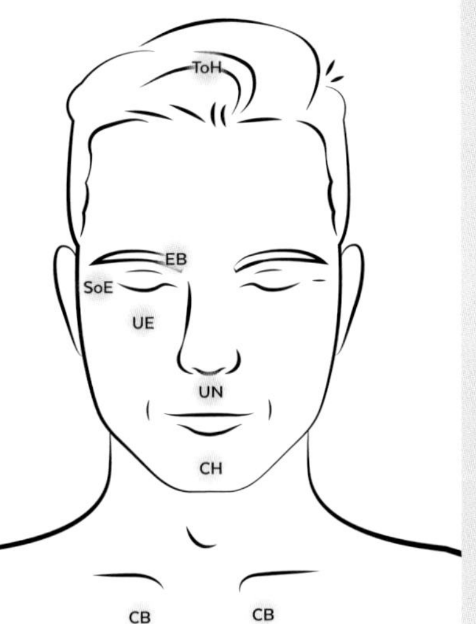

ToH: There are so many parts of me that feel scared, angry and lonely

EB: These parts created from difficult experiences

SoE: That didn't feel safe to be expressed at the time

UE: These parts of me that I've hidden away

UN: They feel ignored, denied and unseen

CH: I've felt unseen, yet I've not seen my whole self

CB: These parts of me are not bad

UA: I've just hidden them away to keep myself safe

IW: I understand now why these parts of me are in shadow

TH: Maybe I've been afraid to view these parts

FF: Maybe I've not known how to support them

MF: Maybe I've not known how to integrate them

RF: It hasn't felt safe to connect with these parts of me

BF: I felt shame of their existence

ToH: Because I didn't understand myself
EB: Because my whole self was not allowed to exist
SoE: I might have felt as though I was too much or too sensitive
UE: Or maybe I wasn't enough for others
UN: But none of this was my fault
CH: I adapted to my surroundings to feel safe
CB: I had to hide these parts of myself, but it's time to let them out
UA: Perhaps it wasn't anyone's fault, as we all have shadows
IW: There's no need for shame; I choose space for all parts of me
TH: I am open to healing and integrating my shadow self
FF: I accept all parts of me as divinely whole
MF: I release labels of 'good' or 'bad' and embrace inner union
RF: I accept the energy and beliefs I've created within me
BF: I am whole, complete and choose to love all of me

ToH: Ego, you've worked so hard to keep me safe
EB: You've protected me so well
SoE: You've created strategies and beliefs
UE: To try to prevent me from being vulnerable
UN: And prevent me from being hurt
CH: These stories and beliefs worked at one time
CB: But now, they are holding me back
UA: From healing, and moving forward
IW: Your strategies are keeping me stuck in the past
TH: I thank you for all you've done for me
FF: And Ego, I ask you now to let go of what doesn't serve me
MF: I ask you to let barriers soften and release
RF: I am safe and secure now
BF: I belong and feel loved

ToH: I give you permission to evolve and support me
EB: To move us forward
SoE: To come back into alignment with our soul's plans
UE: To release uncertainty, judgement and control
UN: To release anger, victimhood and people pleasing
CH: These are strategies I no longer need
CB: I choose now to let them go
UA: Ego, release what is no longer needed
IW: I thank you with compassion and love
TH: We get to choose a new way
FF: Today, we choose compassion, forgiveness and love
MF: We open our hearts to miracles
RF: We trust in our greatness
BF: We trust in the unconditional love of the universe

CHECK-IN

How are you feeling now? Rate yourself on a scale of 0–10. What number are you? Has the intensity dropped? Does your body feel any lighter? Did any memories surface? Feel free to repeat the exercise.

STEP 4:
THE REUNION WITH SELF

This final step guides you to reconnect with your authentic self. Here, we address moments of self-abandonment, explore trust and confidence and strengthen our self-worth and self-love. By releasing outdated beliefs, self-doubt and embracing our true essence, we create space for empowered, authentic living. Each chapter will support you in finding a deeper sense of peace and belonging within yourself, helping you live in alignment with who you truly are. This reunion is an invitation to come home to yourself, grounded, whole and free.

CHAPTER 14

Tapping for Self-abandonment

Every time we say yes to someone or something we don't want to do, we are saying no to ourselves.

Self-abandonment

Many of us are conscious of the times we've felt abandoned by someone in our lives. One of your parents might have travelled a lot for work when you were little; a friend might have decided to join another group when you were in school; or a partner could have recently broken up with you. Whatever the situation and severity, there are many events that occur throughout life that can trigger a sense of abandonment in us.

What we are less likely to be conscious of, however, is all the times we've abandoned ourselves – our true and authentic selves. Self-abandonment is the act of regularly denying our emotions, suppressing our needs and changing our behaviour to please others. In other words, the stress response of people pleasing, or fawning, results in self-abandonment.

We all do this to some degree to keep ourselves feeling safe and to help us to feel loved and included. Have you ever changed your accent depending on which group of friends you were hanging out with? Have you bought an item of clothing just because it was in fashion and all your friends were wearing it? Have you ever faked an illness to get out of something? Have you ever said 'yes' when you really wanted to say 'no'?

SELF-ABANDONMENT IS THE ACT OF REGULARLY DENYING OUR EMOTIONS, SUPPRESSING OUR NEEDS AND CHANGING OUR BEHAVIOUR TO PLEASE OTHERS.

Of the stress responses we can utilize – fight, flight, freeze and fawn (see page 30) – fawning is probably the one we are least conscious of. As an attempt to prevent further traumatic experiences, fawning can lead us to become co-dependent, as we constantly seek external validation, avoid conflict at all costs and, ultimately, dim our own vibrant and shining light.

In extreme cases, it can lead to illness. Sometimes we put ourselves so far down the priority list to please others that we don't notice when our body starts complaining, screaming out for rest and nourishment.

Hidden Suffering

Many of us have no idea that there are repercussions to denying our soul power. Every time we give too much of ourselves to others, repress our own wants and needs for others or dismiss or ignore our own feelings, we are denying a part of ourselves.

On a soul level, this causes the deep pain of internal abandonment and perceived separation. It may feel like there is a great distance between the version of ourselves we share with the world, and our true, authentic soul light and power.

This pain is linked to grief and loss. On a subconscious level, we start accumulating grief. We won't recognize it as grief because it's as if this energy is floating. This grief is not generated or attached to the loss of someone, or because of a particular traumatic experience. We might have started generating these feelings when very young, so have no recollection of when they began to form. These repeated, small acts of self-abandonment often remain hidden from our conscious awareness and are harder to spot when looking back on our lives, too. It can therefore be difficult to bring our awareness to them, to acknowledge, forgive and let go.

Shame and guilt might also be created as we people please because on a subconscious level, we know that we are making decisions that hide our true selves. This could lead to us feeling badly about ourselves and it might reinforce limiting beliefs such as, 'It's not safe to be my true self', 'I'm not worthy' or, 'I'm not enough'.

Self-abandonment is often linked to fear, in particular fear of rejection or abandonment. This is because we felt fear during the initial trauma that led us to fawn in the first place. We then feel fear as we try to say no or enforce a different boundary; or when we try to say how we really feel, ask for what we need and show our true selves. This continual state of fear can keep us stuck in our stress response.

EVERY TIME WE GIVE TOO MUCH OF OURSELVES TO OTHERS WE ARE DENYING A PART OF OURSELVES.

Recognizing Self-abandonment Patterns

Use the table below to help you identify any patterns of self-abandonment in your life. You can then consider these as you tap later in this chapter and connect with the rising emotions. Awareness of your behaviours can help you start to choose differently, so you can authentically honour your needs, speak your truth and create boundaries.

Types of Self-abandonment	Example Behaviour	Emotion/Impact
People pleasing/ fawning	Saying 'yes' when you want to say 'no'	Resentment, anxiety, feeling unimportant or unworthy
Suppression of emotions	Unable to cry or hiding your true feelings to avoid upsetting others	Sadness, shame, tension in throat/ blocked throat
Self-sacrifice	Neglecting your own needs over everyone else's	Burnout, exhaustion, feeling not good enough
Lack of boundaries	Unable to be clear on what is too much, allowing others open access to your energy	Resentment, rage, shame, feeling stuck, anxiety
Seeking external validation	Constantly needing and seeking approval from others	Low self-esteem, desperation, dependence

Unable to accept compliments	Brushing off positive comments, unable to receive or hear nice things about self	Minimizes identity and self-worth, withdrawing into self, feeling unsafe to be seen
Avoiding conflict	Can't express authentic opinion, adapts and accepts other's views over own	Incongruence, shame, resentment, powerlessness
Overworking or perfectionism	Pushing self to physical exhaustion to prove value	Anxiety, imposter syndrome, burnout, disease
Self-criticism	Loud, critical voice, blaming self for mistakes	Reinforced lack of self-worth, shame, low confidence
Changing self to fit in	Adjusting voice, clothes, wants and needs based on others	Inauthenticity, insecurity, grief, shame
Disconnection from needs and wants	No idea what needs and wants are, and doesn't feel safe to ask for them when discovered	Disconnection with body, fragmented self, powerlessness, sadness

The Impact of Self-abandonment

Our bodies are impacted by this heavy energy, which has knock-on effects on our physical health and our ability to cope with future challenging situations. Our emotions are also impacted greatly because we are storing grief, shame, fear and more.

This might make us sensitive to judgements from others because our survival instinct is to belong. We can be hypersensitive to how others interact with us, negatively impacting our relationships, and occasionally causing us to interpret situations in a way that fits with the belief systems and safety strategies we've formed. This then affirms and reinforces those negative beliefs even further.

On an extreme level, this can lead to chronic illnesses, depression, anxiety disorders, resentment, rage, further disconnection and a feeling of emptiness. It therefore impacts the connection to our values, wants and desires, self-worth and ultimately how much we love ourselves. It keeps us stuck in a loop of putting others first, not sharing how we really feel, denying our needs and wants and feeling powerless to change.

Self-abandonment holds us back and keeps us stuck in the past, wedded to times in our lives when it wasn't safe to be our authentic selves. When we are trapped in an invisible prison of trauma, it is very hard to create the life of our dreams.

SELF-ABANDONMENT HOLDS US BACK AND KEEPS US STUCK IN THE PAST.

Being Our Authentic Selves

We can't reconnect with our authentic selves overnight. It's a long process of self-discipline, self-awareness, compassion, forgiveness and love. To help you get started, here are some things you can do to support the journey back to yourself:

- Become conscious of the times that you deny your needs or suppress your feelings and notice any patterns of times when you do this.
- Work on bringing a sense of safety into the body by using tapping and other grounding and somatic practices.
- Engage a therapist, EFT practitioner or additional support to address larger or repetitive traumatic experiences to release the root cause of your self-abandonment; for example, identifying when you first felt unsafe.
- Be a detective to identify what beliefs you hold and observe them with curiosity. For example, 'Oh, isn't it interesting that my mind is telling me not to say that in case she won't be my friend anymore'.
- Ramp up your self-care by prioritizing yourself with nourishment, rest and support.
- Start practising saying 'no' to small things you genuinely don't want to do. Put the 'no' out there without a reason and see how it lands and feels.
- Think about yourself more and others less by placing more importance on your needs over the judgement of others.
- Continually check in to see what emotions are being generated and then acknowledge, forgive and release them using tapping or other tools.

Tapping for Self-abandonment

Tapping helps us get to the root of the pain and suffering we have held in our energy system, acknowledge it and show it compassion, forgiveness and love. In this sequence, we are consciously bringing safety back to the body to turn the belief that 'It's not safe to be me' into something more positive.

Before doing this exercise, take a few minutes to connect with the energy of self-abandonment in your body. What emotions does it bring up when you think about the many times you've denied your true self? Is it sadness, shame, fear? Notice any pains or tension in any areas of your body.

Tune in, find the emotion, give it a colour and location, and rate the intensity from 0–10. Then, take three deep breaths, and follow the set-up steps and sequence, inserting your own wording where this feels right:

SET-UP STATEMENT (TAPPING ON THE SIDE OF THE HAND):

Even though I feel black sadness in my heart because I am now aware of the pain I've caused myself by denying my true self, I choose to forgive, love and accept myself anyway.

Even though I have this black sadness in my heart because I have suppressed myself and neglected my own needs for so long, I choose to forgive, love and accept myself anyway.

Even though I feel black sadness and shame in my heart because I have denied the world of my true self out of fear, I choose to forgive, love and accept myself anyway.

Self-abandonment Tapping Sequence

Commence tapping, starting at the top of the head and going down the points:

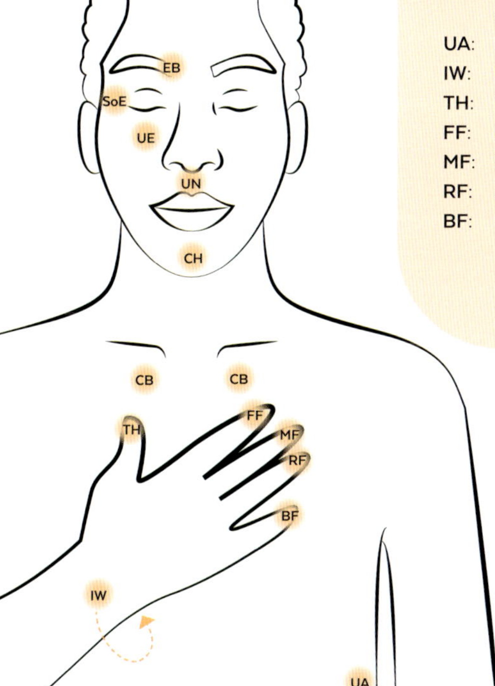

ToH: All this black sadness in my heart

EB: This heavy, black sadness

SoE: I'm now realizing the impact my strategies have had

UE: I realize how much I've hidden my true self

UN: I acknowledge how much I've abandoned my true self

CH: I can see how often I've put others first

CB: And pushed my needs to the bottom of the ladder

UA: I have put everyone else first

IW: I have denied my needs

TH: I have suppressed my emotions

FF: I have dimmed my light

MF: Because I didn't feel safe

RF: And I wanted to feel loved

BF: I wanted to belong

ToH: It makes me so sad to acknowledge this
EB: So sad and heavy in my heart
SoE: Because I see the little child I once was
UE: And I see how much they had to adapt
UN: To please others and keep themselves safe
CH: I feel sorry for my younger self
CB: But I know I was just doing the best I could
UA: I didn't know any other way of receiving love
IW: It was safer to suppress and hide my true feelings
TH: I didn't want to upset those around me
FF: Maybe they couldn't handle my big feelings
MF: Maybe I felt safer doing what I was told
RF: Maybe it wasn't safe to question
BF: Maybe it wasn't safe to state my needs

ToH: Maybe I couldn't find my voice
EB: Maybe I didn't have the support I needed
SoE: Maybe I wasn't encouraged to speak up
UE: I am not that little child anymore
UN: It is safe to speak up and share my needs
CH: It is safe to set boundaries
CB: What if I could release all this hidden pain?
UA: Of all the times I suppressed my true self
IW: What if I could let go of the black sadness in my heart?
TH: What if I could let go of the guilt and shame?
FF: What if I could let go of the fear?
MF: I choose now to let the sadness go
RF: I choose now to let the guilt and shame go
BF: I choose now to let the fear go

ToH: It is safe to let go of old strategies
EB: It is safe to be me
SoE: It is safe to honour my needs as valid and important
UE: It is safe to set boundaries
UN: It is safe to express my needs
CH: It is safe to be seen and heard
CB: I let go of all old patterns and stories
UA: That make me please others
IW: I am important
TH: I let go of the mask I've been wearing
FF: I forgive myself deeply for abandoning myself
MF: I choose to share my true self
RF: I choose to shine my light
BF: I love all parts of me

CHECK-IN

How are you feeling now? Rate yourself on a scale of 0–10. What number are you? Has the intensity dropped? Does your body feel any lighter? Did any memories surface? Feel free to repeat the exercise.

CHAPTER 15

Tapping for Trust and Confidence

Surrender is not a weakness, it is a strength. It takes tremendous strength of intention and grace, to detach from the ego-mind projections and surrender life to the Supreme and to its cosmic unfolding. – *Mooji*

Resistance Versus Surrender

Surrendering is not about giving up. It's about releasing the need to control outcomes that are beyond our reach. Resistance is the opposite of surrender. When we struggle to accept who we are, or the support that is available to us, we create resistance in our energy field. This resistance manifests as dense emotions, limiting beliefs and negative behaviours. Over time, these blocks prevent us from aligning with the natural flow of life force energy that moves through us.

We resist because of past pain. Emotional energy created during trauma or distress, unless acknowledged and released, stays trapped within us. This clouds our judgement, making it difficult to understand the truth of the situation from an elevated perspective. Instead, we operate from a place of fear, clinging to control to avoid potential future pain. The need to be in control gives us a false sense of safety and keeps us stuck in a loop of worry and anxiety. Surrendering, on the other hand, allows us to release that resistance and find peace in uncertainty.

SURRENDERING ALLOWS US TO FIND PEACE IN UNCERTAINTY.

Why We Crave Control

Humans are hardwired to seek control because it offers a sense of security and predictability. It helps us feel certain, safe and powerful. In fact, 'We feel relaxed only when we feel certain about what we know or about what we should anticipate', according to science writer Kostas Kampourakis and philosophy professor Kevin McCain.[1] However, when unexpected events happen that are beyond our control, it's common to experience feelings of helplessness, a loss of self-belief or even self-blame.

Control is particularly important for those who have experienced trauma. If you've lived through situations where you had no control, such as conflict in the home or abuse, or had an accident, you may have developed a heightened need for control to feel safe. In these cases, letting go of control can feel dangerous. But clinging to it creates its own suffering, as we try to manage the uncontrollable and set ourselves up for stress and disappointment.

Control gives us the illusion of certainty. We hold onto it because it makes us feel powerful and protected, yet much of life is beyond our control. In reality, true peace comes from releasing control and embracing the flow of life.

Confidence and Control

Control and confidence often go hand in hand. We feel confident when we believe we have a grip on our circumstances, but when things spiral out of control, that confidence can quickly fade. However, true confidence isn't just about having control. It's about trusting that no matter what happens, you have the inner strength and capability to navigate challenges.

Building confidence requires self-acceptance and trust in your own abilities. When you cultivate self-belief, you release the need to control every outcome because you trust that you can handle whatever life throws your way.

Surrendering Is a Choice

Letting go of the need to be in control is a choice and a process. Surrendering allows us to release resistance and move in harmony with life's natural rhythm. It reconnects us with our inner strength and the flow of universal energy. Surrender doesn't mean passivity. It means making the conscious decision to trust yourself and the unfolding of life. You still act, but you no longer cling to outcomes or stress about what you cannot control. A handy phrase to have on repeat is, 'I detach from the outcome'.

Confidence plays a crucial role here. When we trust in our ability to handle life's ups and downs, we naturally feel more confident in letting go. This is because we've built a foundation of self-trust that assures us we are capable no matter the outcome.

The journey from control to surrender involves building trust in yourself and the universe. If trauma has left you feeling unsafe when there is uncertainty, then cultivating a sense of internal safety is key. Practices that help you ground and centre yourself are essential in this process.

THE JOURNEY FROM CONTROL TO SURRENDER INVOLVES BUILDING TRUST IN YOURSELF AND THE UNIVERSE.

Cultivating Trust, Confidence and Surrender

Trust, confidence and surrender are deeply interconnected. By building self-trust, we naturally become more confident, and that confidence helps us surrender control over the things we can't change. Here are some other techniques you can try alongside tapping to help you on this path.

Breathe: Deep, slow breathing calms your body's stress response. Practicing conscious breathing – inhaling for five seconds and exhaling for five seconds – brings you back to a state of calm, where surrender feels less threatening.

Tone the vagus nerve: The vagus nerve is responsible for regulating the body's stress response. Toning it by making a long 'oooooo' sound on your exhale activates the parasympathetic nervous system, which promotes relaxation and trust (see page 30).

Mindful grounding: In moments of anxiety or overwhelm, bring your attention to what you can see, hear, feel, taste and smell in your environment. This grounding practice helps you stay connected to the present, where you are safe and supported.

Assess control: Make a list of what you can and cannot control in your current situation. Acknowledging what is beyond your influence helps you let go of unnecessary worry and focus on what you can actively change.

Affirm your confidence: Repeat affirmations such as, 'I trust in my ability to navigate this challenge' or, 'I am confident in my strength to handle what comes'. These statements remind your mind and body of your inner power and reduce the fear that drives control.

Strengthen resilience: Remind yourself of the challenges you've already overcome. Your resilience is evidence of your inner strength, and acknowledging this can boost your confidence in facing future uncertainties.

Confidence in Trusting the Universe

Trusting in a higher power or the universe requires both confidence in yourself and faith in the bigger picture. When you believe that life is unfolding for your highest good, even in difficult times, you can release the need to control everything and focus instead on aligning with your true self. This trust opens the door to unexpected opportunities, miracles and personal growth.

Letting go of control doesn't mean giving up on your goals or desires. It means trusting the process. As you build confidence and trust, you allow the universe to support you in ways that go beyond what your mind can imagine. You make space for the flow of life to guide you toward your authentic path and limitless potential.

Living from a baseline of trust and confidence not only enhances your emotional wellbeing, but also your physical and mental health. Reducing stress, releasing negative beliefs and embracing uncertainty opens the door to peace and joy. When you trust in yourself and surrender to life's flow, you cultivate the resilience to navigate whatever challenges arise.

As you continue this journey, bear in mind that trust, confidence and surrender are not destinations, but practices. There will be times when you naturally slip back into old habits of needing to be in control, and that's okay. What's important is to return consistently to your practices of grounding, trust and self-compassion.

Tapping for Trust and Confidence

As the need for control is rooted in feeling a lack of safety, tapping is the perfect tool to support a release of the resistance and tension that brings. As we tap, we send signals of safety to the nervous system, allowing tension to reduce, and cortisol and adrenaline to subside (see page 30). Focusing on letting go of the fear of uncertainty will help boost confidence in yourself and the natural flow and rhythm of life.

Before doing this exercise, take a few minutes to connect with the energy of fear, uncertainty or lack of trust in your body. Is there something you are worrying about, or an area in which you lack confidence? Notice any pains or tension in particular areas.

Tune in, find the emotion, give it a colour and location, and rate the intensity from 0–10. Then, take three deep breaths, and follow the set-up steps and sequence, inserting your own wording where this feels right:

SET-UP STATEMENT (TAPPING ON THE SIDE OF THE HAND):

Even though I feel yellow anxiety in my stomach because my desire to control is so strong, I choose to trust I am capable and strong.

Even though I am afraid to let go and surrender, I choose to trust that I am safe and supported.

Even though I doubt myself and have trouble trusting the universe, I understand this is a result of trauma, and I choose to forgive, love and accept myself anyway.

Trust and Confidence Tapping Sequence

Commence tapping, starting at the top of the head and going down the points:

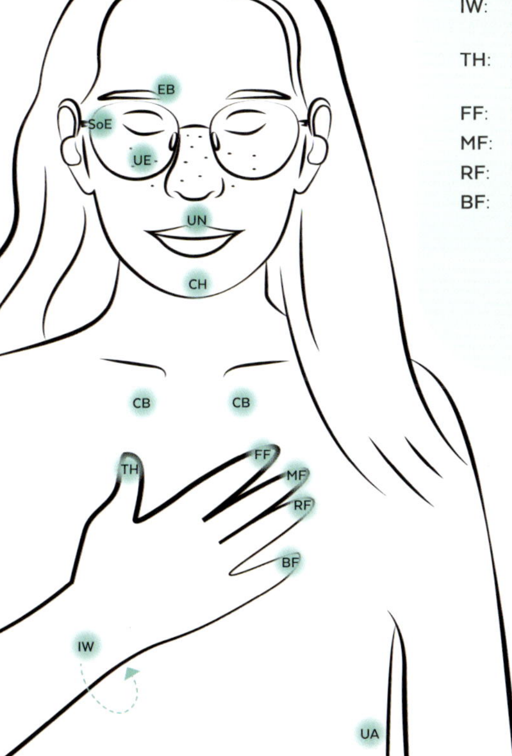

ToH: This yellow anxiety in my stomach
EB: All this uncertainty
SoE: I worry so much about the future
UE: I think of every eventuality
UN: I am always trying to gain control
CH: I find it so hard to trust
CB: I find it hard to let go
UA: I feel I need to control everything to feel safe
IW: I'm afraid of what will happen if I let go
TH: I don't always trust things will work out
FF: Because of what my past tells me
MF: Because I've been hurt so much
RF: Trusting makes me feel nervous
BF: Surrendering makes me feel unsafe

ToH: I find it so hard to trust and feel safe
EB: I feel powerless, burdened by doubt and stress
SoE: My need for control is rooted in avoiding pain
UE: My anxiety keeps me on edge, afraid of the unknown
UN: These fears weigh me down
CH: What if I could release this need for certainty?
CB: What if I could let things unfold as life intends?
UA: What if I could detach from the outcome?
IW: I choose to remember I have survived my hardest days
TH: I choose to believe that I can cope
FF: I choose to believe I am capable
MF: I choose to believe in myself
RF: I can handle whatever life throws at me
BF: I am stronger and more capable than I realize

ToH: I am ready now to trust in myself and life more
EB: I am ready to detach from the outcomes
SoE: I choose to live in the moment more
UE: I choose to stop worrying about all the possibilities
UN: I choose to remember how brave I am
CH: I forgive myself for these limiting behaviours
CB: Because I've just been trying to keep myself safe
UA: I've needed safety so badly
IW: Driving my deep need for control
TH: None of that is my fault
FF: It's a by-product of past experiences
MF: Where I haven't felt safe
RF: I honour everything I've been through
BF: I love and accept all experiences

ToH: I allow my body to feel safe even as I let go
EB: I allow my body to surrender
SoE: I allow my mind to detach from the outcomes
UE: I release the need for control
UN: And choose confidence in my resilience
CH: I choose to trust myself and the universe
CB: I choose to accept all that comes my way
UA: Is meant for me on some level
IW: I can cope with whatever is my divine plan
TH: My divine plan is what is meant for me
FF: I am excited about where life takes me
MF: I am open to miracles
RF: I am open to limitless opportunities
BF: I am divine potential and I've got this

CHECK-IN

How are you feeling now? Rate yourself on a scale of 0–10. What number are you? Has the intensity dropped? Does your body feel any lighter? Did any memories surface? Feel free to repeat the exercise.

CHAPTER 16

Tapping for Self-worth and Self-love

The journey back to your true self starts with the transformative power of unconditional love.

Self-worth and Self-love

Self-worth and self-love underpin everything that you have learned in this book so far; the journey back to your true self starts with the transformative power of unconditional love. The very nature of reading my words and tapping along is an act of self-love, because on some level, you feel worthy of feeling this unconditional life-force energy.

Right at the heart, in every cell of your body, in every layer of your energy field, love is within you. You are love. Our previous experiences have created resistance to knowing, understanding and feeling this. Our traumas shape us with emotions, beliefs and behaviours that ultimately are there to protect us and keep us safe.

Resistance takes the form of sabotage, addictions, negative actions and reduced potential, putting a chokehold on the universal life-force energy of love that naturally flows to and through us. It is not our fault, and for some reason beyond our current understanding and control, we are exactly where we are meant to be in this moment, painful suffering and all. Time will surely tell, and understanding will come at some point. But, for now, we work on acknowledging, accepting, forgiving, trusting, letting go and loving.

RIGHT AT THE HEART, IN EVERY CELL, IN EVERY LAYER OF YOUR ENERGY FIELD, LOVE IS WITHIN YOU.

Understanding Self-worth

It can feel uncomfortable for some of us to say, 'I am worthy'. That discomfort is resistance and significant of an inner belief of not deserving. As we explored in Chapter 7, our early childhood experiences shape this the most, as if we grow up feeling unloveable or unwanted, then walls of protection will build in our energy field. This will perpetuate the feelings of being unloveable as we will not allow ourselves to feel loved. A lifelong struggle with self-acceptance and self-love awaits if we don't feel deserving.

Self-abandonment, as discussed in Chapter 14, disconnects us from our authentic selves to gain acceptance and approval, yet it chips away at our sense of self and ultimately our self-worth. Our sense of inner value is often conditional to achievements, success and behaviour, perpetuating our people-pleasing behaviours and linking our self-worth to external validation, and other people's judgements of us.

Self-worth is in fact innate and not reliant on other people's opinions. Reclaim your self-worth and you will realize how important and valuable you are to the very fabric of life itself. It isn't conditional to any actions; you are worthy simply because you exist.

Understanding Self-love

Self-love is not merely an abstract concept; it is an active practice that invites us to embrace acceptance, compassion and forgiveness as vital pathways toward nurturing our authentic selves. When we approach ourselves with these qualities, over time we free ourselves from the harsh judgements and the critical voice of ego that distorts our sense of worth.

Embracing conscious self-love actions benefits us greatly in multiple ways. It builds our strength and resilience so we can navigate life's challenges with grace and confidence. This changes how we respond to life, allowing us to see opportunities and gifts all around us. It connects with the practice of gratitude, mindfulness and presence.

Think of self-love as your inner cheerleader who backs you to pursue your dreams, chase those goals and push you beyond your comfort zone. Our self-belief and boundaries are strengthened as we understand how to set limits that honour our time, energy and personal values.

A healthy foundation of self-worth is essential for cultivating self-love, and unconditional acceptance of all parts of us is what reconnects us back to our true selves. Living authentically allows us to embrace our imperfections, expand our capacity for compassion and nurture our inner strength. As we nurture self-love, we unlock the door to feeling more love and to living a more authentic, empowered and fulfilled life.

The Self-love Reflection

The following exercise will help you deepen your self-awareness and foster self-love through daily reflection. Try to dedicate 5–10 minutes each day to this practice, preferably in the morning or before bed.

You will need a journal and pen for this reflection. You may also choose to use matches or a lighter, a candle, essential oils and soft music.

1

Sit quietly in a comfortable space where you won't be disturbed.

2

Create an inviting atmosphere, for example by lighting a candle, playing soft music or using essential oils. Allow yourself to feel relaxed and present in this safe space.

3

Reflect on the following questions:

- What are three things I appreciate about myself today?
- What do I need to let go of from today?
- What did I do today that made me feel proud or happy?
- How can I show kindness to myself tomorrow?

4

Write down your answers in a journal dedicated solely to your self-love journey. This can help solidify your thoughts and feelings, creating a tangible record of your growth.

5

After journalling, close your eyes and visualize a warm, loving light within and surrounding you. Imagine this light filling you with warmth, acceptance and compassion. Allow yourself to feel this love deeply, recognizing that you are worthy of it.

6

Finish your session by saying a self-love affirmation out loud. For example, 'I am enough just as I am', 'I embrace my imperfections and celebrate my uniqueness' or 'I deserve love and kindness from myself'.

7

At the end of each week, review your journal entries. Identify patterns in your reflections, notice what made you feel good and think about small actions you can take to nurture your self-love in the upcoming week.

Tapping for Self-worth and Self-love

By loving and respecting our whole selves unconditionally, we create a solid foundation that supports us through life's challenges. We can prioritize ourselves, live authentically, and stop judging ourselves and comparing ourselves to others. This helps us to weather any storm.

This tapping sequence is designed to be done regularly. It works deep in your subconscious and your heart to help you let go of past experiences, old narratives and limiting beliefs. Use this sequence to shift your perspective and boost self-love.

Before doing this exercise, take a few minutes to connect your sense of self-worth and self-love. Do any memories immediately come to mind that may have caused you to not feel worthy or not feel loved? Notice any pains or tension in particular areas.

Tune in, find the emotion, give it a colour and location, and rate the intensity from 0–10. Take three deep breaths, and follow the set-up and sequence, inserting your own wording as you wish:

SET-UP STATEMENT (TAPPING ON THE SIDE OF THE HAND):

Even though I don't feel deserving of an abundance of joy and love in my life, I choose to forgive, love and accept myself anyway.

Even though I have this black emptiness in my heart because I've been unable to love myself unconditionally, I choose to work on my self-love, compassion and acceptance.

Even though I've struggled to love and accept myself flaws and all, today I choose to open myself up to change.

Self-worth and Self-love Tapping Sequence

Commence tapping, starting at the top of the head and going down the points:

ToH: This dark emptiness in my heart
EB: This numbness inside of me
SoE: Sometimes I feel so numb to joy
UE: I'm unable to let love in
UN: I don't feel worthy of that love
CH: I've never felt truly worthy of love
CB: I haven't experienced unconditional love
UA: There was always a condition
IW: I received love if I was a 'good' child
TH: If I did well at school
FF: If I never caused trouble
MF: If I said yes to everything
RF If I kept the peace
BF: If I bottled everything inside

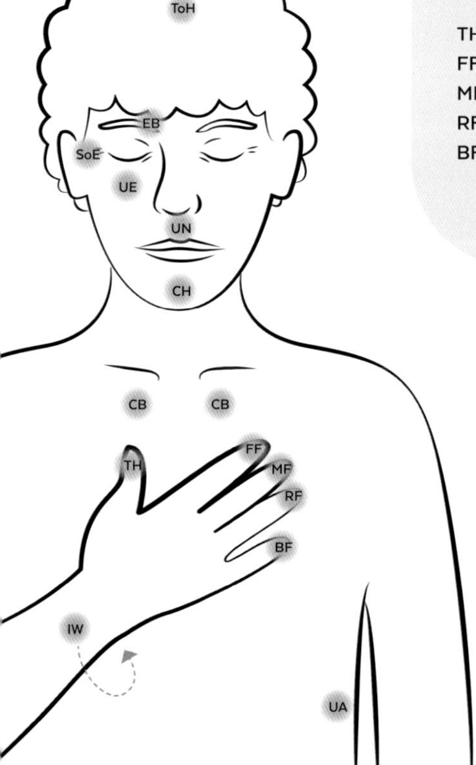

ToH: I've struggled to feel truly lovable and enough
EB: I crave unconditional love and acceptance
SoE: I compare myself to others and feel like I fall short
UE: I often feel unworthy and hold myself back
UN: This fear of not being good enough weighs on me
CH: I've learned to self-sabotage and doubt myself
CB: I'm afraid to speak my truth or show my real self
UA: I hold on to guilt, shame and a need for control
IW: I tend to please others, even when I want to say no
TH: Deep down, I struggle to trust and feel deserving
FF: Living this way feels so dark and heavy
MF: I know life isn't meant to feel this way
RF: It was no one's fault I didn't get what I needed
BF: They couldn't give me what they never received

ToH: Deep down I know I'm enough
EB: I see my inner child and understand their pain
SoE: I choose to release any self-blame, guilt and shame
UE: I did the best I could at the time
UN: My past doesn't define me anymore
CH: I'm ready to release these old beliefs
CB: I am worthy of love, kindness and abundance
UA: I choose to accept all parts of me, just as I am
IW: I know I am whole, capable and enough
TH: I am ready to let go and change
FF: I choose to accept I am not perfect
MF: I choose to accept all of my imperfection
RF: I choose to let go of all of these doubts about myself
BF: It is safe to let go of all my pain now

ToH: It is safe to let go of the past and move forward
EB: I choose to love myself unconditionally
SoE: I choose to feel worthy
UE: I choose to know I am good enough
UN: I am more than enough
CH: I am exactly what I need
CB: I open my heart to all the love that surrounds me
UA: It is safe to be me in every way
IW: It is safe to love myself completely
TH: It is safe to have faith in myself
FF: I back myself in every way
MF: I know I am worthy and good enough
RF: I accept and claim my worthiness now
BF: I accept that I am unconditional love

CHECK-IN

How are you feeling now? Rate yourself on a scale of 0–10. What number are you? Has the intensity dropped? Does your body feel any lighter? Did any memories surface? Feel free to repeat the exercise.

Final Thoughts

As we come to the end of this journey together, remember that tapping is not just a tool but also a bridge that brings you back home to yourself. Whether you've been working through fear, resistance or the need to be in control, the path always leads back to love, trust and confidence. Tapping is your invitation to reconnect with your inner truth, gently releasing the old stories, beliefs and emotions that no longer serve you.

The core of this journey is self-love, the foundation of all healing. By honouring every part of your journey, whether it's pain, doubt, joy or triumph, you open the door to deeper compassion and understanding. Tapping gives you the freedom to forgive yourself for holding onto past fears or limiting beliefs while allowing trust and surrender to flourish.

Take a moment to revisit the self-ratings you noted at the start of this book on page 9. Now, after completing this journey, rate yourself again. Have you noticed any shifts? Reflect on changes beyond the numbers. Consider your levels of anxiety and whether your boundaries have become clearer and more defined. Are you feeling more confident and self-assured? Have you become more comfortable asking for what you need and expressing your authentic voice? Has your critical voice quietened and your intuition strengthened?

Final Tips

It's important to remember that healing is an ongoing process. Consult a practitioner such as myself for the deeper release work, and know that you can use tapping yourself whenever you need it. Whether you're navigating daily stress, feeling emotionally overwhelmed or in need of a confidence boost, these practices can be tailored to your busy schedule. Try the suggestions below.

Daily micro-tapping: Take five minutes in the morning to tap through a few rounds while setting an intention for the day. This helps ground your energy and sets the tone for a more mindful approach to whatever arises.

On-the-spot relief: Use tapping in the moment whenever intense emotions arise. Even just tapping on the side of the hand or collarbone points and repeating a simple phrase like, 'I am safe right now' can help shift your state and restore calm.

Nightly release: End your day by tapping through any emotions that built up during the day, letting go of tension, and preparing your body for restful sleep.

Tapping is always there for you, whether as part of a structured daily routine or as a go-to tool when you feel overwhelmed. Use the sequences throughout this book as often as you need, trusting that each time you tap, you're stepping further into self-love, trust and confidence.

You have all the tools you need to thrive. Now, embrace your inner strength and tap into the limitless potential that's always been within you.

Additional Resources for Inner Healing

Over the course of my healing journey, I have tried a wide variety of healing modalities, techniques and support. Here are some of the things I've found really useful alongside tapping to help me understand myself better, let go and improve my energy frequencies. You can find descriptions of some of these other modalities in Chapter 5.

- Bach flower remedies
- Essential oils
- Homeopathy
- Kinesiology
- Healy microcurrent frequency device
- Akashic Record readings
- Reiki and Rahanni
- Sound healing
- Breathwork
- Journalling
- Meditation and visualization
- Reflexology
- Massage

I love reading self-help books and the following authors have been my favourites. These writers offer a range of approaches, from trauma healing and mindfulness to self-compassion and personal empowerment, making them great complementary tools for you to explore alongside tapping.

Anna Mathur
Dr Bessel van der Kolk
Brené Brown
Dr Bruce Perry and Oprah Winfrey
Dr Clarissa Pinkola Estés
Dr David Hamilton
Eckhart Tolle
Emma Mumford
Gabby Bernstein
Gregg Braden
Dr Gabor Maté
Dr Joe Dispenza
Karl Dawson and Kate Marillat
Kirsty Gallagher
Louise Hay
Mark Wolynn
Meggan Watterson
Dr Peta Stapleton
Rebecca Campbell
Rhonda Byrne
Sophie Bashford
Dr Wayne Dyer

References

Chapter 2: Tuning in to Energies

1. Big Think (2014) 'Max Planck: "I regard consciousness as fundamental..."' Available at https://bigthink.com/words-of-wisdom/max-planck-i-regard-consciousness-as-fundamental/ (Accessed: 21 Nov 2024).

2. Piaget, J. (1973) *To Understand is to invent: the future of education.* Grossman Publishing.

3. Rozin, P. and Royzman, E. B. (2001) 'Negativity bias, negativity dominance, and contagion', *Personality and Social Psychology Review*, 5/4, 296–320.

Chapter 3: How to Tap

1. Mayo Clinic (2023) *Chronic stress puts your health at risk.* Available at: https://www.mayoclinic.org/healthylifestyle/stress-management/in-depth/stress/art-20046037 (Accessed: 21 Nov 2024).

2. Stapleton, P. et al. (2020) 'Reexamining the effect of emotional freedom techniques on stress biochemistry: A randomized controlled trial' *Psychological Trauma: Theory, Research, Practice, and Policy*, 12/8, 869–877.

3. Church, D. et al. (2022) 'Clinical EFT as an evidence-based practice for the treatment of psychological and physiological conditions: A systematic review' *Frontiers in Psychology*, 13.

Chapter 4: Tapping into Your Emotions

1. Davey, S. et al. (2021) 'Where is emotional feeling felt in the body? An integrative review' *PLOS One* (Accessed: 21 Nov 2024).

Chapter 5: Tapping for Grounding

1. Bettersleep (2019) *The science behind Solfeggio frequencies* Available at: https://www.bettersleep. com/blog/science-behind-solfeggiofrequencies (Accessed 21 Nov 2024).

2. Unknown, *Solfeggio scale effect on the mind and body* Available at: https://static.secure.website/wscfus/9158863/uploads/Solfeggio_for_Ponder_Final.pdf (Accessed: 21 Nov 2024).

Chapter 7: Tapping for Grief and PTSD

1. Church, D. (2014). 'Reductions in pain, depression, and anxiety

symptoms after PTSD remediation in veterans' *EXPLORE*, 10/3, 162–9.

Chapter 8: Tapping for Forgiveness

1. Wade, N. et al. (2013). 'Efficacy of psychotherapeutic interventions to promote forgiveness: a metaanalysis' *Journal of Consulting Clinical Psychology*, 82/1, 154–70.

Chapter 9: Tapping for Guilt, Shame and Blame

1. Brown, B. (2021) *Atlas of the Heart: Mapping Meaningful Connection and the Language of Human Experience*. Vermilion.

Chapter 12: Tapping into Motherhood

1. Mathijssen, J.J.P. et al. (2024) 'Transition to motherhood: adverse childhood experiences, and support from partner, family and friends' *Maternal and Child Health Journal*, 28, 1242–1249.

Chapter 15: Tapping for Trust and Confidence

Quote by Mooji is copyright © Mooji Media Ltd 2024, www.mooji.org.

1. Kampourakis, K. and McCain, K. (2019). *Uncertainty: how it makes science advance*. Oxford University Press.

Index

Acknowledgements

This book has been with me since 2019, and I am so proud to finally deliver it to you.

It would not have been possible without the unwavering support of my family, who have cheered me on every step of the way. My deepest gratitude to my husband, Dave, who carved out space for me to write, soothed my doubts and has been the steady rock grounding me throughout this journey.

To my children, my greatest inspiration: our daughter Alice, whose guiding light in heaven gave birth to this book, and our sons Casper and Josh, my profound teachers. This book is a legacy for all of you.

A heartfelt thanks to my agent, Kizzy Thompson, my editor, Louisa Johnson, and the team at Octopus Publishing Group for believing in this project and helping me bring it to life so beautifully.

To my friends, clients and EFT practitioner trainees, thank you for your encouragement and for inspiring all my work to date.

Finally, to you, my readers and supporters: thank you for inviting this journey into your life. I walk alongside you in this work, growing and healing together.

About the Author

Sarah Tobin is an Irish-born EFT practitioner, trainer and writer now living on the south coast of the UK, near the beach, where the rhythm of the sea inspires her work. She is dedicated to helping others navigate their emotional landscapes, heal from trauma and reconnect with their inner strength and true selves. With years of experience supporting individuals and groups, she blends her expertise in tapping, mindfulness and somatic practices to empower personal transformation.

As a mother, Sarah draws deeply on her own journey of love, loss and healing to inspire her work. She is passionate about creating tools, resources and workshops that make emotional wellbeing accessible to all. When she's not working with clients or writing, she enjoys spending time with her family, walking her dog and exploring life's quieter moments of joy and connection.

If you'd like to work with Sarah, you can find details about her offerings at www.tappingwithsarahtobin.com, where she provides one-on-one sessions, group workshops and tailored EFT programmes to help you find healing and emotional clarity on your pathway to becoming your authentic self.